Y0-EAF-765

THE LOVE THAT MOVES THE STARS

Also by James C. Howell:

Yours are the Hands of Christ: The Practice of Faith

Servants, Misfits & Martyrs: Saints and their Stories

THE LOVE THAT MOVES THE STARS

Reflections on the Stained Glass of Davidson United Methodist Church

James C. Howell

Leslie B. Rindoks
BOOK DESIGN

LORIMER & PINE PRESS *Publishers*

Text copyright © 2000 James C. Howell
Design copyright © 2000 Leslie B. Rindoks

Conceptual window designs are the sole property of
The Willet Stained Glass Studios © 1994

All rights reserved. No part of this book may be
reproduced or transmitted in any form without
written permission.

Printed in USA

Library of Congress Control Number: 00-092600

Howell, James C.

ISBN 0-9704651-0-6

For Those Who Have Inspired & Illuminated

Ever since the day our stained glass windows were installed, I have wanted us to publish this book, and many are to be thanked. Leslie Rindoks, a genius when it comes to design, color, and excellence, put it all together marvelously, as she does in all her work. Larry Ligo and the rest of the sanctuary interiors committee of the church thought through the design carefully and wisely, and did not settle for less than the best. Crosby Willet of Willet Studios was a gentleman and friend through the design process of the windows, and Jane Collins, the artist who conceived of the images, was the creative force that still shimmers in each window. Stephanie Chesson shot the photographs of the stained glass on a long but successful Fat Tuesday. Tish Signet, Jayne Braxton, Peter Krentz and Jennifer Gilomen read the text and made helpful suggestions. And of course we are grateful for our church family at Davidson United Methodist Church for sharing the vision of worshipping with vitality in a place that appeals to all the senses.

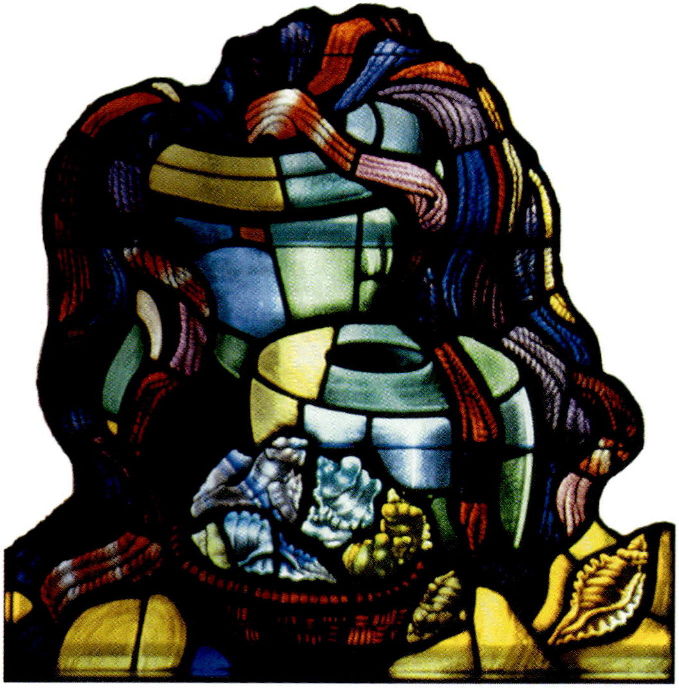

CONTENTS

PROLOGUE		ix
CREATION	In Him was Life	1
BAPTISM	The Dove Descending	5
LORD'S SUPPER	He Took Bread	9
CRUCIFIXION		
	Man of Sorrows	13
	Unrevealed Until its Season	19
	You Will Find Rest	21
	What Can I Give	23
	Broken Places	25
	The Sower Went Out	27
SAINTS		
	Lydia, Paul & Silas	29
	Francis & Clare of Assisi	33
	Martin Luther	37
	John Wesley & Francis Asbury	41
	Mother Teresa & Martin Luther King	45
REVELATION	Light of the World	49
EPILOGUE	How the Light Gets In	53
WINDOW DONORS		55

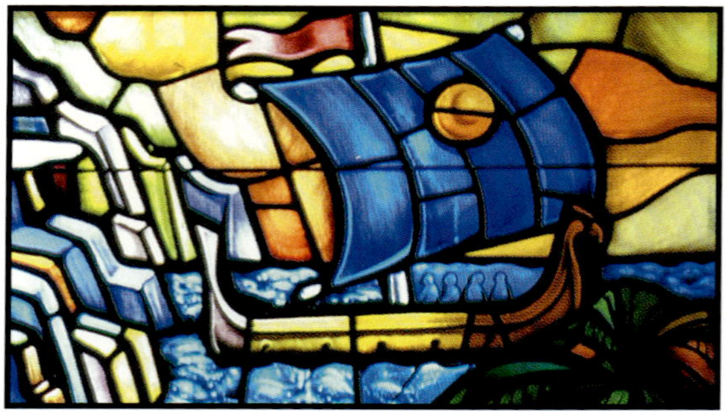

Prologue

I worship in a place, a room, with hundreds of people on Sunday morning. Then I slip into that same space by myself, when nobody is looking except God, on a weekday afternoon or on a Saturday morning. For me, the sanctuary is holy, palpably pervaded by the presence of God, reminding me of God's presence in every other room and space.

This room is graced by a marvelous series of stained glass windows. Like worshippers since the Middle Ages, I can bathe in light filtered through glass that translates simple sunlight into colors. Each small piece is a thing of beauty, unique in color and shape. The artist has deftly arranged those separate individual pieces into images, of tone and hue that shift depending on the hour and season.

Each window paints a powerful image, and all the windows together narrate God's story, which surrounds not only those who sit in this room, but all of us throughout our lives. I need these images of a dove, a grain of wheat, a cross, a saint, for during most of my life I am bombarded with titillating images from television, billboards, the internet, magazines — images that muddy the waters of my soul. Holy images in glass remind me who I am, whose I am, where I am going.

Henri Nouwen said, "A spiritual life in most of our energy-draining society requires us to take conscious steps to safeguard that inner space where we can keep our eyes fixed on the beauty of the Lord."

Images in art help us pray. At times I just cannot pray. I am too tired, too restless. But I can look, wait, contemplate, letting my frazzled mind be bathed in God's love, my fragmented self healed and carried along the stream of grace. And I may even be surprised by what I glimpse with my interior eye. St. Francis, who is very much present in this room with me, used to pray before a romanesque crucifix in a little broken down church in Assisi called San Damiano. One day as he gazed at the cross, Jesus spoke to him and said, "Go and rebuild my church, for as you can see it is falling into ruin." When our eyes are fixed on the beauty of the Lord, we will intuitively envision the beauty of serving the Lord.

Through these pages, you will see these windows, their images, the beauty. I offer some reflections, just my own ruminations, which I pray will prod you to tilt your head and heart and see the story from a fresh angle. So look, keep looking, and see, not just with your eyes, but with your heart.

*Water surged
and
color blossomed.*

In Him was Life

Facing east, toward the rising sun, is a window pulsating with energy, a witness to the story of creation. We all wonder: Why are we here? What's the point of my life? Lots of questions gravitate toward the beginnings of the universe: How did we get here? Scientists have gazed through powerful telescopes and detected subtle shifts in the light spectrums from stars, trying to discern how the universe came to be. Their best guess is that some fifteen billion years ago there was a rapid release of startling amounts of energy, which over time have gathered into galaxies, supernovas, nebulae, black holes, solar systems, comets, mountains, oceans. The huge expanse of America does not even qualify as a speck of dust in a universe with, not just millions of continents or even stars, but millions of galaxies, each stretching across a space so large that light, which travels far faster than you can blink your eye, requires countless centuries to make it from one end to the other.

Is all this here by accident, some cosmic quirk of fate? Are we spinning mindlessly across that expanse into sheer darkness? Einstein called God "the old one," and refused to believe that God was "playing dice" with the universe. Before there was even such a thing as time, God, who chooses not to be alone, who cannot help giving birth to wonders, flung this universe into being, and has nurtured it like a mother would her baby from millennium to millennium. Consider the odds of life as we know it coming to be. If the charge on an electron, or the force of gravity, or the energy at the core of the sun, were one hundredth of one percent different, life could not exist. We would not exist.

By the word of the Lord the heavens were made,
and all their host by the breath of his mouth.
He gathered the waters of the sea as in a bottle,
He put the deeps in storehouses.

— Psalm 33:6-7

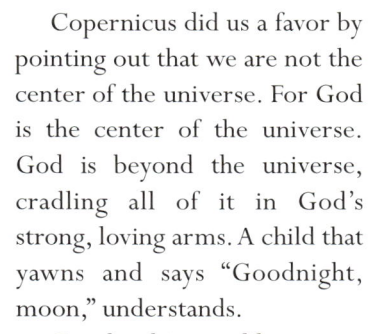

Copernicus did us a favor by pointing out that we are not the center of the universe. For God is the center of the universe. God is beyond the universe, cradling all of it in God's strong, loving arms. A child that yawns and says "Goodnight, moon," understands.

For the skies are like a great canopy stretched out above us, with pin-holes here and there, each emitting a pencil ray of the glory of God. The star we see is truly ancient light, that began racing toward us while we slept, before our ancestors slept, hastening to this moment before the first human ever looked up. To God, that unfathomable stretch of time is comprehended in an instant, held together by what Dante called "the Love that moves the sun and the other stars."

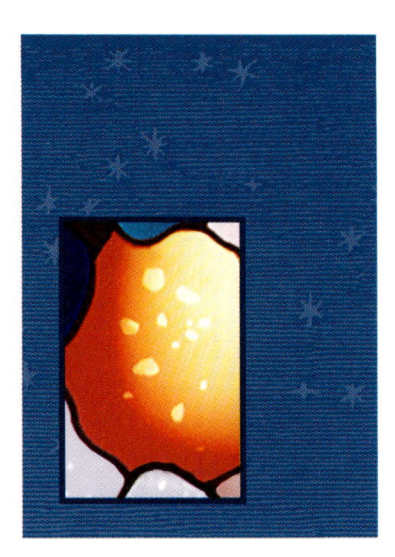

But God is not just around or outside the universe. God gets involved. On the single miniscule planet called earth, the array, the variety, the splendor of what God has made dumfounds us. Porcupines, forests, minnows, pinecones, daffodils, sharks, preying mantises, redwoods, centipedes, hummingbirds, squash, weeping willows, hyenas, ostriches, lizards, watermelons. Nature is profligate, unceasing in its diversity. God exhibits some bizarre sense of humor in nature – as if there is absolutely nothing God won't try at least once. The least we can do, given the generosity of such a God, is to get outside and look around – and notice.

The advent of life on earth is startling, and merciful. Imagine a molten surface, rocky here and there, smoke hovering – and yet miraculously some pioneer molecules, issued from the energy of God's own heart, bonded and grew and became life. Water surged and color blossomed. Every creature, every thing that breathes, crawls, chirps, growls, is one more voice in the great chorus of praise to the one in whom we live and move and have our being. If you want good television preaching, watch those shows that visit the haunts of the jackal, the nests of the eagle, the depths of the ocean.

Last and luckiest of all, creatures we know as people survived. Some synapse fired in the brains of the first man and woman worthy of the name and they lifted their eyes upward and gave thanks to a Being they could not see but knew had to be responsible for it all.

Our glory is the privilege of living in God's creation. Our honor is that God became our brother in Christ, taking on flesh, living in the world we share, ennobling the world, and us, by his presence. The least we can do is notice.

The glory of our life in this world does not magically emerge from inside us. This is all a surprising gift, described by John, who looked up and back into the hazy recesses of time and saw the truth of reality:

In the beginning was the Word,
and the Word was with God,
and the Word was God.
He was in the beginning with God;
all things were made through him,
and without him was not anything made
that was made.
In him was life,
and the life was the light of men.
The light shines in the darkness,
and the darkness has not overcome it.

– JOHN 1:1-5

And cannot overcome it. We can trust God who is our home.

When I consider your heavens, the work of your fingers,
  the moon and the stars which you have established,
Who are we that you are mindful of us?
Yet you have made us little less than God,
  and you crown us with glory and honor.

— Psalm 8

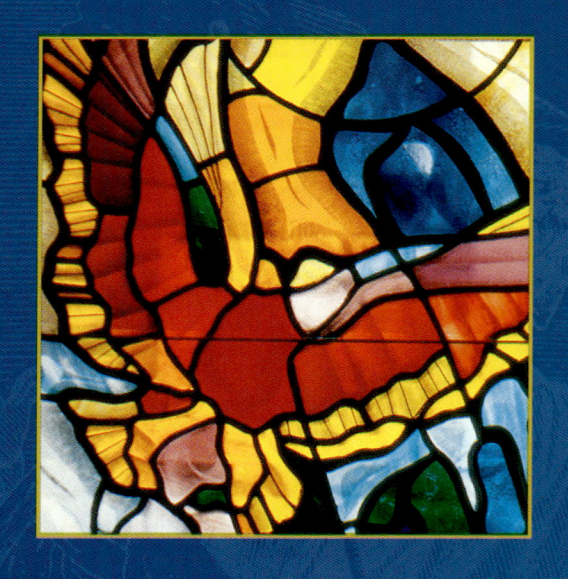

And a voice came from heaven, "You are my beloved son. With you I am well pleased."

The Dove Descending

To the sides of the altar are a pair of windows, highlighting two Sacraments of the church. We begin every service of Baptism by saying, "The Church is of God, and will be preserved to the end of time." For twenty centuries, the Church has baptized people, infants, children, adolescents, adults, in every language, in every place, immersing them in massive pools, sprinkling their heads. With joyful simplicity, we do as Christ told us to do.

And when we are baptized, we do what Christ did. Just as he embarked on his ministry, "*Jesus came from Nazareth and was baptized by John in the Jordan. When he came up out of the water, immediately he saw the heavens opened and the Spirit descending upon him like a dove. And a voice came from heaven: 'You are my beloved son. With you I am well pleased'*" (Mark 1:9-11).

Ask any child what water is for, and she will answer, "To drink when I'm thirsty," and "To bathe in when I'm dirty." Jesus needed no forgiveness. So why was he baptized? Karl Barth said Jesus was not being theatrical, but that he was in fact baptized for the forgiveness of sins: Jesus did not let our sins remain our sins but, determined to be our brother, took our sins on himself, and came to the Jordan afflicted by all our waywardness and affliction, just as he took our misery to the cross at the end of his ministry.

On the cross Jesus cried out, "I thirst." What irony! This is the man who asked the woman for water from Jacob's well (John 4), but then told her she would continue to be thirsty until she knew him, for he was and is the "living water." Baptism's powerful symbol is water, for it is the grace of God that we are desperately thirsty for. And the only thing that can quench our thirst is something we cannot buy, or earn, or even entirely figure out (Isaiah 55:1-11). God's great gift to us is free.

This is why we baptize infants. Do they know or remember God? Have they done anything yet to achieve their status as God's precious children? Of course not. Infants are utterly and wonderfully dependent on the gentle care of parents to feed, hold, dress, and cherish them. And so it always must be with us and God. Water brings life. Water softens the parched ground, and our hard hearts.

Without water, living things cannot grow, and without God's grace we wither and die. Water surges, subsides, cools, is breathed by the creatures of the deep.

God's Spirit descended on Christ like a dove. That same Spirit of God, at the dawn of time, "brooded over the face of the waters" (Genesis 1:2). After the forty days of rain ceased, Noah sent out a dove, who searched and plucked out a lone sign of life and hope, an olive leaf. That same Spirit of God came down like the rush of a mighty wind, "like tongues of fire" (Acts 2:2-3), and the disciples, so sullen and in despair, were catapulted out into the streets to change the world. C.S. Lewis's good friend, the novelist Charles Williams, wrote a history of the Church appropriately titled *The Descent of the Dove*.

God's Spirit descended on Christ, with a declaration: "You are my beloved child." Since Christ is our brother, since Christ did what he did so we could be set right with God, then we dare to hear in that voice from heaven God's very word to

"There is living water within me…"

— St. Ignatius

us. Every one of us should hear God say, very personally, "You are my beloved child."

Perhaps this is hard to hear, or seems just unbelievable. That's why Martin Luther repeatedly urged us to remind ourselves each day that "I am baptized!" Remember who you are. Remember whose you are. Your worth does not rest on the great things you achieve, or your good looks or clever brilliance. Your worth rests on this descending dove, and this freely given image of God etched indelibly on your self. And so we are thankful. Not prideful, and never saying "I've earned what I've got." The dove descends where it will, with power, gently.

St. Augustine said that a sacrament is a "visible word." The word made visible in the water of Baptism is that God is "love." God says "I love you." Think about the implications of this visible word. God gives us everything – and asks for everything. C.S. Lewis wrote, *"You asked for a loving God: you have one. The great spirit you so lightly invoke is present: not a senile benevolence that drowsily wishes you to be happy in your own way, not the cold philanthropy of a conscientious magistrate, nor the care of a host who feels responsible for the comfort of his guests, but the consuming fire himself, the Love the made the worlds, persistent as the artist's love for his work and despotic as a man's love for a dog, provident and venerable as a father's love for a child, jealous, inexorable, exacting as love between the sexes."*

If God's love is akin to what we hope for in families and among friends, then that love, this descending dove, calls us into a great congregation of God's people in every place, in every century, in the past, now, in the future. Through Baptism we discover ourselves to be the brothers and sisters of Simon Peter and Mary the mother of Jesus, of Paul, Silas and Lydia, of Francis and Clare of Assisi, of Martin Luther, of the Wesley family, of Mother Teresa, Martin Luther King, not to mention our parents, grandparents, siblings, children and friends, and an almost infinite host of others whose names may have been forgotten by us but most certainly not by God.

Hildegard of Bingen wrote, *"The Holy Spirit is life-giving life, universal mover and the root of all creation, refiner of all things from their dross, brings forgiveness of guilt and oil for our wounds, is radiance of life, most worthy of worship, wakening and reawakening both earth and heaven."* Will we let the Spirit do its work, give us life, awaken us to love? The yearning is there. We all sense it in the marrow of our souls. As Ignatius of Antioch said, "There is living water in me, water that murmurs and says within me, 'Come to the Father.'"

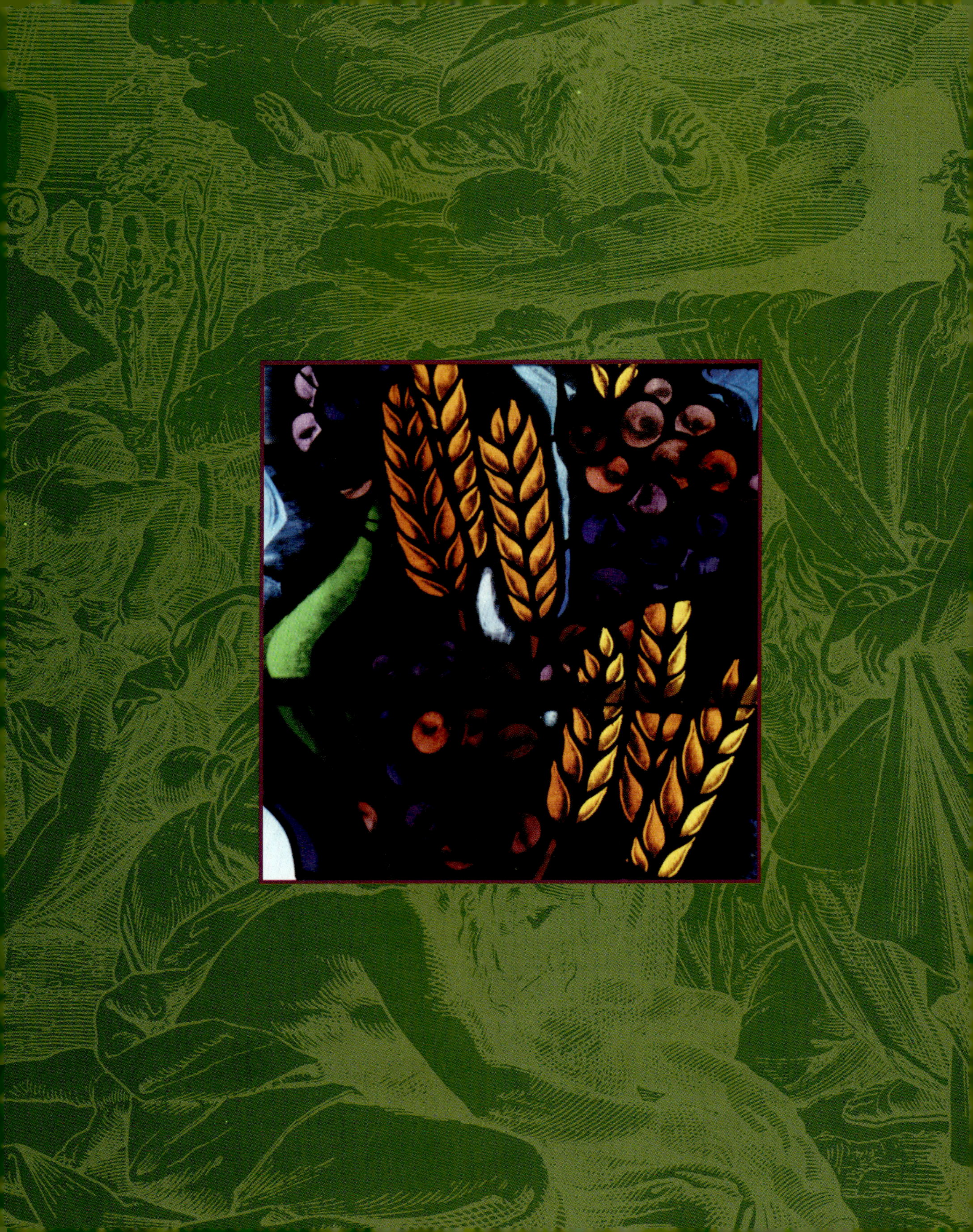

He Took Bread

"Why is this night special above all other nights?" So asks the son in the Jewish family's ritual on the evening of Passover. The answer, of course, is that Passover celebrates God's miraculous deliverance of the people of Israel from bondage in Egypt. In celebration, the finest male lamb is slaughtered and eaten, along with unleavened bread, and other symbolic foods.

It was Thursday, just after sundown. The moon was full, a "harvest" moon. Jesus had ridden into Jerusalem on a donkey to shouts of "Hosanna!" — and he had panicked the authorities by bodily throwing the moneychangers out of the temple precincts. Jesus sensed his time was short. And so with great irony he sat down to the Passover with his disciples, his friends, that night special above all other nights, a night of festive celebration, yet a night fraught with agony for Jesus, his untimely end looming so near.

"He took the bread, and blessed it" (Mark 14:22). Jesus certainly "blessed it" by using the traditional Jewish prayer over the loaf for Passover: "Blessed are you, O Lord our God, King of the universe, who brings forth bread from the earth." In the Old Testament, Passover is interlaced with the feast of Unleavened Bread. In fact, at the Passover meal, bread prepared without yeast (*mazzoth*) is eaten, as a reminder of how the Hebrews fled Egypt in such haste the women forgot their leaven. But Unleavened Bread was also a festival of thanksgiving for farmers. Millennia before the advent of sprinklers, fertilizers, pesticides, and government subsidies, farmers planted and then knelt daily on dry, rocky soil, pleading with the heavens to yield some rain. When, or if, the rains came, and the wheat or barley grew, the people knew their survival hinged on forces beyond their control. And so they were grateful.

The Lord's Supper has traditionally been called the "Eucharist", a word that means thanksgiving. Thanksgiving is not congratulating ourselves for having so much. Rather, giving thanks means having an attitude of dependence upon God for even the simplest joys: a piece of bread, a roof, the rain, another breath. Gratitude is virtually passé in our culture, where we work, earn, "deserve" everything. The bread at Holy Communion reminds us that every good and perfect gift comes from God (James 1:17). We are not our own. The question for us is neither "What is mine?" nor "What do I have coming to me?" but rather this word from one of the Psalms Jesus and the disciples would have sung that night: "What shall I render to the Lord for all his bounty to me?" (Psalm 116:12).

Wheat and barley were precious in Israel. When the crop finally was ready, when the first sickle struck the first ripened stalk, that grain was not immediately baked into bread, however hungry a family might have been for even a few crumbs. Rather, that first fruit of the earth was offered back to God as a sacrifice. Something precious. Mother Teresa once said, *"Giving is not just what you can live without, but what you can't live without, or don't want to live without, something you really like. Then your gift becomes a sacrifice, which will have value before God. Giving until it hurts is what I call love in action."*

To answer "What shall I render for all his bounty?" the disciples would have continued and sung these lyrics: "I will lift up the cup of salvation and call on the name of the Lord" (Psalm 116:13). After they ate the bread, Jesus "took the cup, and when he had given thanks he gave it to them." Again, he would have used the traditional Jewish prayer over the Passover wine: "Blessed are you, O Lord our God, King of the universe, who brings forth fruit from the vine." If we contemplate the bread and the wine, we may ask why Jesus chose these basic elements, and with startling courage said "This is my body, and this is my blood." Simple, the staff of life, basic staples, bread and wine. At some level we may imagine that bread, as it is broken in two, is a matchless symbol of a body, just as Jesus said "The bread I give for the life of the world is my body" (John 6:51). Surely no more potent symbol for blood could have been found than wine. Frederick Buechner even said that *"Unfermented grape juice is a bland and pleasant drink...but it is a ghastly symbol of the life blood of Jesus Christ, especially when served in individual antiseptic, thimble-sized glasses. Wine is booze, which means it is dangerous and drunk-making. It makes the timid brave and the reserved amorous. It loosens the tongue and breaks the ice. It kills germs. As symbols go, it is a rather splendid one."*

But there is more. At the Lord's Supper, this "Eucharist," people who are separated are drawn around a single table. We become one family. In church, people who might normally never see each other become one body because of our fellowship with the risen Christ through this sacrament. Ponder the grapes. In a vineyard, there are thousands of grapes, each with a slightly different shape, its own peculiar color and shading. But as the wine is made, each grape ceases to be an individual. Each is poured out to become a part of the wine, no longer isolated, but flowing together as one. Without Christ we are isolated, even lonely individuals, on our own in the world. But by the miracle of the grace of God, we become one, part of something bigger than ourselves. What a privilege! What gratitude we may have in our hearts.

We call it "communion," not merely because we commune with God, but because we are drawn into communion with each other. The Lord's Supper is all about fellowship. Jürgen Moltmann said that Holy Communion takes place "on the basis of an invitation which is as open as the outstretched arms of Christ on the cross."

For what we all have in common is a hunger for God. Jesus continues to stretch out his hands to us, and offers nothing less than his love, his very self, saying, "I am the bread of life. He who comes to me shall not hunger, and he who believes in me shall never thirst" (John 6:35). The homesickness we all feel is an ache for him, for that living bread, the only food that can satisfy the hungry soul. The bread of life, the body of our Lord.

"Come, sinners, to the gospel feast;
Let every soul be Jesus' guest.
Ye need not one be left behind,
for God hath bid all human kind.

Come Holy Ghost, Thine influence shed,
And realize the sign;
Thy life infuse into the bread,
Thy power into the wine."

— Charles Wesley

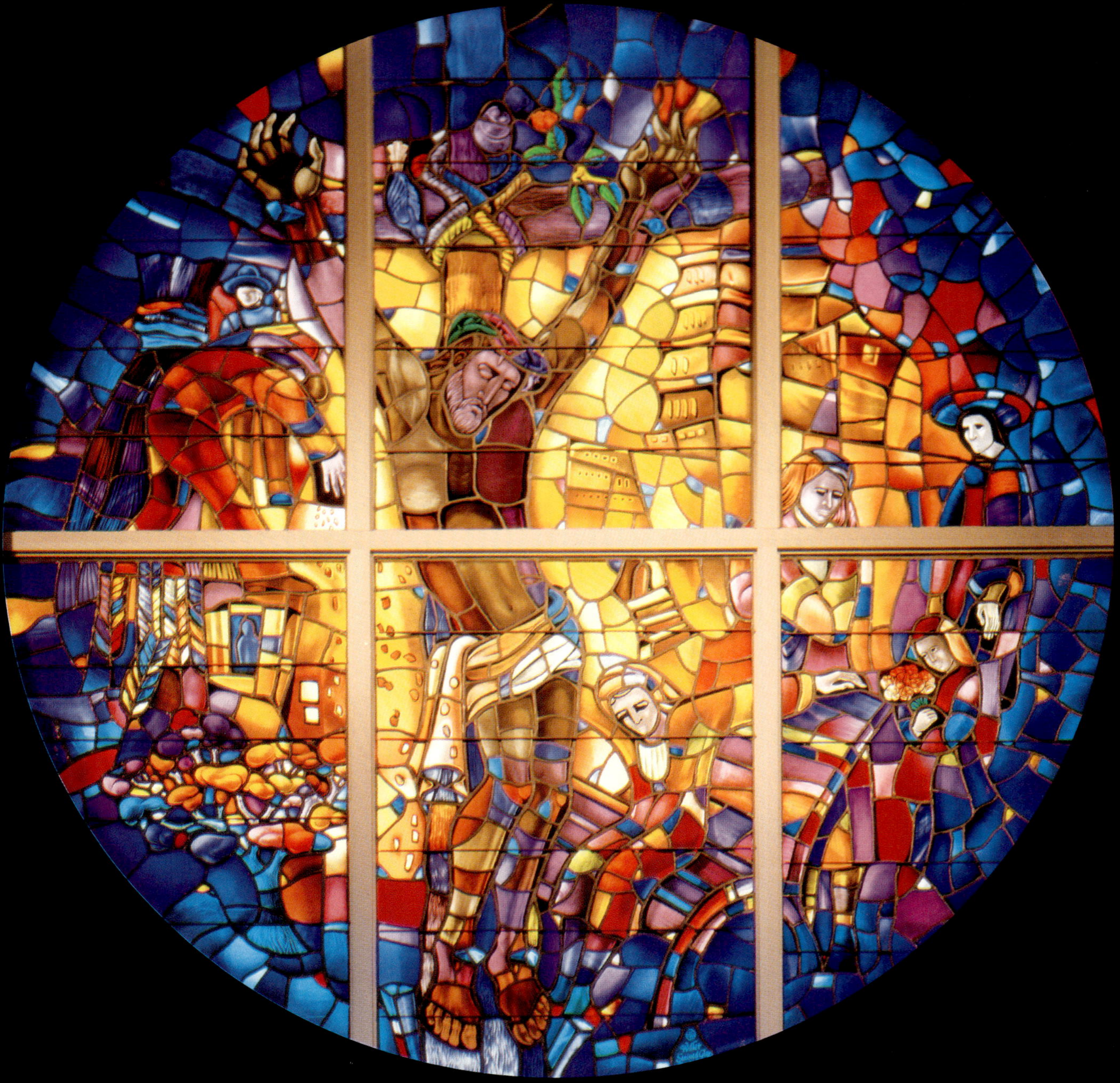

Man of Sorrows

The focal point of the sanctuary, and in fact the focal point of spiritual life, is Christ, whose sorrowful death is the heart of the Gospel. The New Testament shares with us four Gospels, four theological biographies about Jesus. In all of them, the life and ministry of Jesus moves along at a rapid pace, with Jesus walking here, taking a boat there, very active, almost as if he had to get it all in quickly, for his time was short. But then in every Gospel, the pace slows to a crawl once Jesus arrives in Jerusalem. The last days of his life are told in painstaking detail. Everything hangs in the balance, and we wait, and watch.

Finally on that last Friday, after a sham trial with trumped up charges, Jesus, who was all love, all goodness, all devotion to God, the Jesus who had healed and done mighty wonders was executed in a gruesome manner, nails driven through his wrists and feet, a lance piercing his side, a shameful form of capital punishment reserved by the Romans for the most despicable of criminals. Onlookers mocked. The disciples fled for fear and shame. But it was in that moment that God was glorified, that the true mission Jesus had been on all along was revealed. Hidden in his suffering was the simple revelation of the love of God. The centurion in charge of the execution saw Jesus die, and was startled into saying "Truly this was the Son of God" (Mark 15:39).

Jesus' last words are noteworthy. He cried out in dereliction, "My God, my God, why have you forsaken me?" (Mark 15:34), a harrowing but hopeful prayer for all who feel abandoned by God. Looking on those doing the killing, he had mercy on them: "Father, forgive them, for they know not what they do" (Luke 23:34). To a common thief he pledged eternal fellowship: "Today you will be with me in Paradise" (Luke 23:43). To his beloved disciple he gave responsibility to care for his mother. With amazing calm he breathed his last: "Father, into your hands I commit my spirit" (Luke 23:46). And with profundity said, "It is finished" (John 19:30) – not just his life, but his mission of salvation for us all.

The apostle Paul spoke of the crucifixion twenty years later:

*For the word of the cross is folly to
those who are perishing,
but to us who are being saved it is the power of God.
We preach Christ crucified.
For the foolishness of God is wiser than men,
and the weakness of God is stronger than men.*
— 1 Corinthians 1:18-25

Indeed, the Cross proves to be a window flung open into the very heart of God. God's heart reveals itself to be one of pure compassion, immense, immeasurable love, unstinting mercy. On the cross, Jesus took on his own heart all our sin, all our false starts, all the debris of our lives, all our hurts, those inexplicable tragedies, our rejection, our grief, all human hopelessness, every tear.

God is not aloof from our suffering. Rather, God is closest to us when we suffer, so that we never suffer alone, so that our death is ennobled, joined to God's gracious mercy. The cross, if it was constructed of olive wood, the most abundant wood near Jerusalem, must have been less artistically exquisite than the crosses we erect in our churches. Olive wood bends and twists, with knots and crooked joints. The cross of Christ may be imagined as a gnarled shaft of a tree, bent in our spiritual imagining in the shape of a question mark, God's question mark looming over our existence, reminding us that things are not as they seem — yet also a question mark looming over all cynicism and despair. What disaster is so great that God has not entered into it fully and known it entirely? God put his loving arms around our pain. God filed his own painful protest against evil. And God announced in his own flesh and blood that evil does not have the final say. God has the last word, and that last word is one of hope, one of redemption.

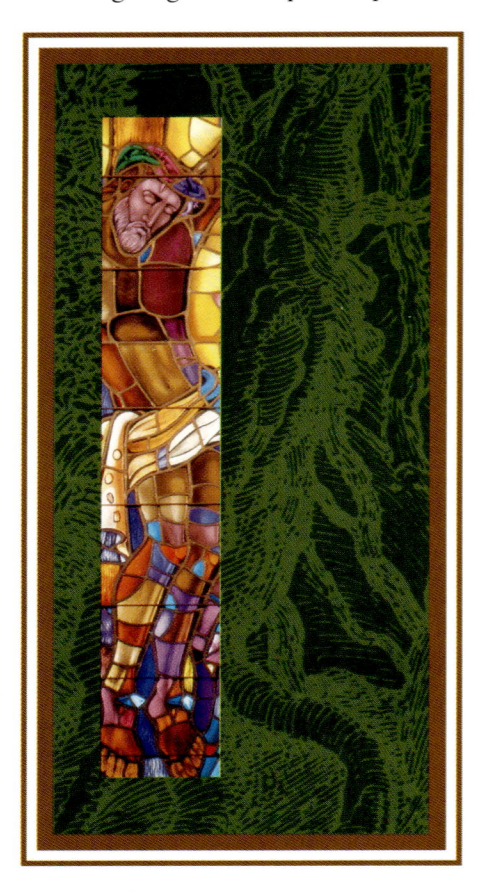

Think again of the gnarled cross as a question mark. Jesus in his suffering stands forever as God's challenge to us, questioning our values, our foolish quests, our lack of compassion, our self-centeredness. The cross is God's reminder that you don't resolve conflict by force but by love, that integrity is costly but is ultimately honored by God, that those with clout are more likely to be in the wrong than the weak, that beauty is only skin-deep.

Most importantly, the crucified Christ invites us to love. In the final months of his life, St. Francis of Assisi prayed these remarkable words:

My Lord Jesus Christ,
Two graces I ask of you before I die:
the first is that in my life I may feel,
*   in my soul and body, as far as possible,*
that sorrow which you, tender Jesus,
underwent in the hour of your most bitter passion;
the second is that I may feel in my heart,
*   as far as possible,*
the abundance of love with which you,
son of God, were inflamed,
so as willingly to undergo such a great passion
*   for us sinners.*

Many of our beloved hymns help us feel that passion. The ancient passion chorale:

*O sacred Head, now wounded, with grief and shame weighed down,
now scornfully surrounded with thorns, thine only crown:
how pale thou art with anguish, with sore abuse and scorn!
How does that visage languish which once was bright as morn!*

Or Isaac Watts's timeless lyrics:

*When I survey the wondrous cross
on which the Prince of Glory died,
my richest gain I count but loss,
and pour contempt on all my pride.
See from his head, his hands, his feet,
sorrow and love flow mingled down.*

*Did e'er such love and sorrow meet,
or thorns compose so rich a crown?
Were the whole realm of nature mine,
that were an offering far too small;
love so amazing, so divine,
demands my soul, my life, my all.*

Christians in every time and place have found refuge in the crucified Jesus, love in his face, hope in the darkest moments. When he stretched out his arms on the cross, he stretched out God's love to embrace the world, and you, and me.

On Good Friday, Christians read the poignant, awesome words from the Old Testament that are fraught with meaning and invite us to consider the passion of Christ:

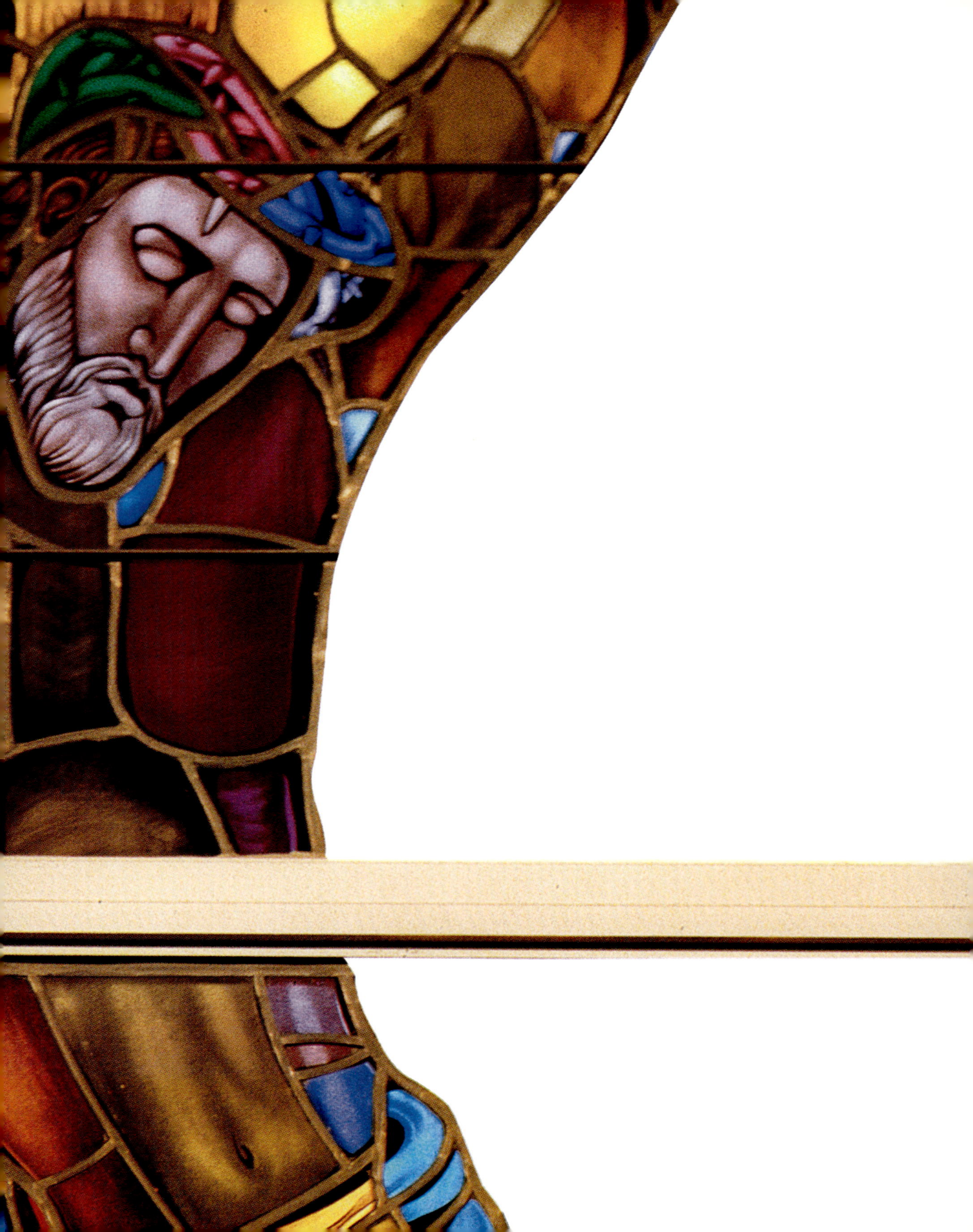

Behold, my servant shall be lifted up.
Many were astonished at him —
his appearance was so marred,
beyond human semblance,
and his form beyond that of the sons of men —
so shall he startle many nations.
Kings shall shut their mouths because of him;
Who has believed what we have heard?
And to whom has the arm of the Lord been revealed?
he had no form or comeliness that we should look at him,
and no beauty that we should desire him.
He was despised and rejected by men;
a man of sorrows, and acquainted with grief;
and as one from whom men hide their faces.
He was despised, and we esteemed him not.
Surely he has borne our griefs and carried our sorrows.
Yet we esteemed him stricken,
smitten by God, and afflicted.
But he was wounded for our transgressions,
he was bruised for our iniquities;
upon him was the chastisement that made us whole,
and with his stripes we are healed.
All we like sheep have gone astray;
we have turned every one to his own way;
and the Lord has laid on him the iniquity of us all.
He was oppressed, and he was afflicted,
yet he opened not his mouth;
like a lamb that is led to the slaughter,
and like a sheep that before it shearers is dumb,
so he opened not his mouth.
And they made his grave with the wicked
and with a rich man in his death,
although he had done no violence,
and there was no deceit in his mouth.
Yet he bore the sin of many,
and made intercession for transgressors.

— Isaiah 52:13-53:12

Unrevealed Until its Season

Hardly noticeable, a bird is perched on the crossbeam. Karl Barth once said that the Holy Spirit prefers anonymity, prefers to stay in the background, for the Spirit's joy is to draw our attention, not to the Spirit, but to God's son, to Jesus Christ. When Jesus, on the cross, cried out "My God, my God, why have you forsaken me?" we may be certain that the agony of that cry was heard nowhere more clearly or painfully than in God's own heart.

For the mystery of the Christian faith is that God is not just God, but that God is a community of three, Father, Son, and Holy Spirit, and it was that community that suffered most acutely during the crucifixion. Just as the Spirit "brooded" over the chaos at creation and brought forth life, so at the agony of Jesus, the Spirit must have brooded in sorrow over the death of this one who came to give life. That same Spirit who descended at the Jordan river to declare, "This is my beloved Son in whom I am well pleased," no doubt hung its head in grief over the beloved Son.

If God is a community of three, then the whole point of the active life of God is to invite us into that circle, so we may become sharers in God's own life of love and fellowship. All our cries, when we suffer in any way as Christ did, grieves the Spirit. But notice the inner meaning of our crying out to God: "When we cry, 'Abba! Father!' it is the Spirit himself bearing witness with our spirit that we are children of God… I consider that the sufferings of this present time are not worth comparing with the glory that is to be revealed to us… The whole creation has been groaning in travail until now. The Spirit helps us in our weakness. We do not know how to pray as we ought, but the Spirit himself intercedes for us with sighs too deep for words" (Romans 8:15-26).

For the Gospel tells us that there is hope in the midst of sorrow, life in the midst of death. Some of our college students went to Nicaragua and stumbled upon a miracle. Barbed wire, coiled atop a wall, a symbol of fear, anger, death – but defiantly, joyfully, a vine had woven itself through the barbed wire, and a rose was in bloom.

The cross on which Jesus was crucified would have been an olive tree, not burnished and sanded and shiny, but just raw wood. Surely something green still grew from this instrument of death. In 1985, Natalie Sleeth wrote the exquisite "Hymn of Promise," one of the most popular new songs in our hymnal. Shortly after she finished composing it, her husband Ronald was diagnosed with cancer. He asked her to have "Hymn of Promise" sung at his funeral – and it moves all of us who are living and dying with its hopeful melody.

In the bulb there is a flower, in the seed, an apple tree;
in cocoons a hidden promise: butterflies will soon be free!
In the cold and snow of winter there's a spring that waits to be,
unrevealed until its season, something God alone can see.

There's a song in every silence... there's a dawn in every darkness...
In our end is our beginning; in our time, infinity;
in our doubt there is believing; in our life, eternity.
In our death, a resurrection; at the last, a victory,
unrevealed until its season, something God alone can see.

Consider the ancient Saxon poem, *The Dream of the Rood*. In this imaginative poem, the cross tells its story. Once it had been a sapling growing in the woods, but men hacked it down and dragged it to a hill, and hewed its branches, all so a criminal could be put to death. "But there came to me no criminal, but the young hero, the Son of God." The cross, the "rood" trembled but dared not bend. It was pierced by the nails, and drenched by the hero's sweat and blood. It held him for hours, and then the hero's body was taken down. They cut down the cross and threw it into a pit. But when he who had hung upon the cross was raised, men came and uncovered the cross and decked it with gold and precious stones and paid it great honor. "So now I tower high and mighty under the skies, having the power to heal all who will bow before me."

You Will Find Rest

At the foot of the cross we see a woman bowed before Jesus. Who is she? When Jesus was crucified, almost all his followers had fled, save a tiny handful of women. Mary, his mother — and artists have struggled for centuries to depict the unspeakable grief of this mother watching the lifeblood she had given her son drain out of him. Mary Magdalene — his surprising disciple who was delivered from a host of inner demons. A couple of others, including Jesus' aunt, also named Mary, the wife of Joseph's brother Clopas.

Perhaps she is someone else, one of the innumerable host for whom Jesus died, women and men facing sorrow, hopelessness, loneliness. Her head is bowed, perhaps not in prayer so much as in disappointment. Walker Percy reminded us that:

If Christ brings us new life, it is all the more remarkable that the Church, the bearer of this good news, should be among the most dispirited institutions of the age.

We are not so much like Prometheus, scaling the heights and stealing the fire of the gods. Rather, we are like Sisyphus, condemned to roll a massive stone up a mountain, only to get near the top and have it slip and roll down once more. Or we are like Atlas, doggedly hoisting the whole world on our shoulders — only to discover it's heavy, far more than we can bear.

And so we are exhausted. The poor, the homeless, know this weariness. Just to sit on some park bench for a little respite is a meager pleasure. Is she sitting on a park bench? Or is the bench really a pew? She sits, head bowed, weary, tired — and can she hear the melody?

*The main emotion of the adult Northeastern American who has all the advantages of wealth, education, and culture is **disappointment**.*

   Work is disappointing …
   Marriage and family life are disappointing …
   School is disappointing …
   Politics is disappointing …
The churches are disappointing, even for most believers.

Softly and tenderly Jesus is calling,
calling for you and for me;
See on the portals he's waiting and watching,
watching for you and for me.
Come home, come home;
ye who are weary, come home;
Earnestly, tenderly, Jesus is calling, calling,
O sinner, come home!

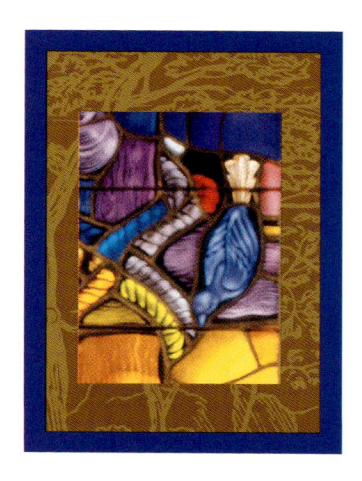

Jesus, after all, had said,

Come to me, all who labor and are heavy laden,
　and I will give you rest.
Take my yoke upon you, and learn from me.
For I am gentle and lowly in heart,
　and you will find rest for your souls.
　　　　　　　　　　　— Matthew 11:28-29

Perhaps if she would lift her head she would see just beyond Jesus' face that dove, peering down in grief, in love. Just before he died, Jesus had said he would send a "comforter" (John 14-16).

We are not always ready for this comforter. Luther said, "The name Comforter means that he must discharge his office at no place save where there is no comfort to be found, and where comfort is needed and longed for. Therefore he cannot comfort hard heads and haughty hearts."

The kind of comfort the dove and the crucified one give is to draw us out of our isolation and loneliness. This woman is above all else alone. But the Spirit and Christ would not have her remain so. Just as they are a community of love, so they invite her into their love. Jesus' last words were "I am with you always" (Matthew 28:20).

But it is not just that Christ is always with her, or me. Rather, we are invited into a community. Jesus looked down from the cross and saw his mother. With amazing tenderness, he spoke to his beloved disciple and said, "Behold your mother" — and to his mother he said "Behold your son" (John 19:26-27). He made provision for her care, that she not be left alone, but find a new home.

This is the Church. A new home for the lonely, the weary, the disappointed. A new family of love, encouragement, hope, and service. A circle, a community, just as God is a community. Who else needs to be drawn in?

WHAT CAN I GIVE?

Nestled against the window support, clinging yet turning away, is another woman. Why does she turn her head away? Is she ashamed? Does she need forgiveness? Healing? We all hesitate, and for our own unique reasons. Throughout the Bible, God calls people, but they hold back. Jeremiah was too young. Isaiah wasn't good enough. Moses was not able to accomplish what God wanted. The disciples didn't understand. Mary had never been with a man. Her mood may reflect one of Sarah McLachlan's lyrics: "I fear I have nothing to give, and I have so much to lose here in this lonely place…"

"But with God, nothing is impossible" (Luke 1:37, Genesis 18:14). Whatever our past, whoever we are, wherever we have been, however we have been hurt, we are welcomed with open arms by Jesus, and by the Church. Perhaps you have heard of the healing shrine in France called Lourdes. Back in 1858, a fourteen year old girl, named Bernadette Soubirous, had a series of visions of the virgin Mary. Shortly afterwards, thousands of gallons of water began to flow from the rocks where little Bernadette spoke with Mary. Thousands claimed to have been cured in its streams.

A friend of mine spent a couple of weeks in Lourdes several years ago. When she returned, I asked her, "Did you see any miracles?" She said, "Oh yes, every day." "Every day? Tell me!"

She explained: "Every day at Lourdes, no matter who you are, or where you are from, or what's wrong with you, you are welcomed, and loved."

And so it is for all of us. Hope surprises us. Perhaps the woman's head is not just turned away from the cross. Perhaps she is noticing the child beside her. A little girl with flowers. Jesus said "Unless you become like children, you will never enter the kingdom of heaven" (Matthew 18:3). Indeed, Joseph Cardinal Bernardin said, "When Jesus opened his arms to embrace a little child, and when he opened his arms wide on the cross to embrace the whole world, it was one and the same."

A childlike faith. Not a childish faith. But childlike. When children want to express their love, their gratitude, they don't spend hundreds of dollars on something of great value. Instead, they give something of even greater value. They spy out some beauty on God's good earth, like wildflowers, and they cut them and bring them to you. There is a hymn we sometimes sing at Christmas:

> *In the bleak midwinter, frosty wind made moan,*
> *earth stood hard as iron, water like a stone;*
> *snow had fallen, snow on snow...*
> *Our God, heaven cannot hold him, nor earth sustain...*
> *In the bleak midwinter, a stable sufficed*
> *the Lord God Almighty, Jesus Christ.*
> *Angels and archangels may have gathered there,*
> *cherubim and seraphim thronged the air;*
> *but his mother only, in her maiden bliss,*
> *worshipped the beloved with a kiss.*

And then the most poignant stanza:

> *What can I give him, poor as I am?*
> *If I were a shepherd, I would bring a lamb;*
> *if I were a Wise Man, I would do my part;*
> *yet what I can I give him:*
> *give my heart.*

Perhaps this child not only comes with her own gift of her own heart. Perhaps she also is the one who brings the one who is hesitant for so long. Luther knew why God came as a child: "God became small for us in Christ. He showed us his heart, so he might win our hearts." It was Wordsworth who rightly said, "A child, more than all other gifts that earth can offer to declining man, brings hope with it, and forward looking thought."

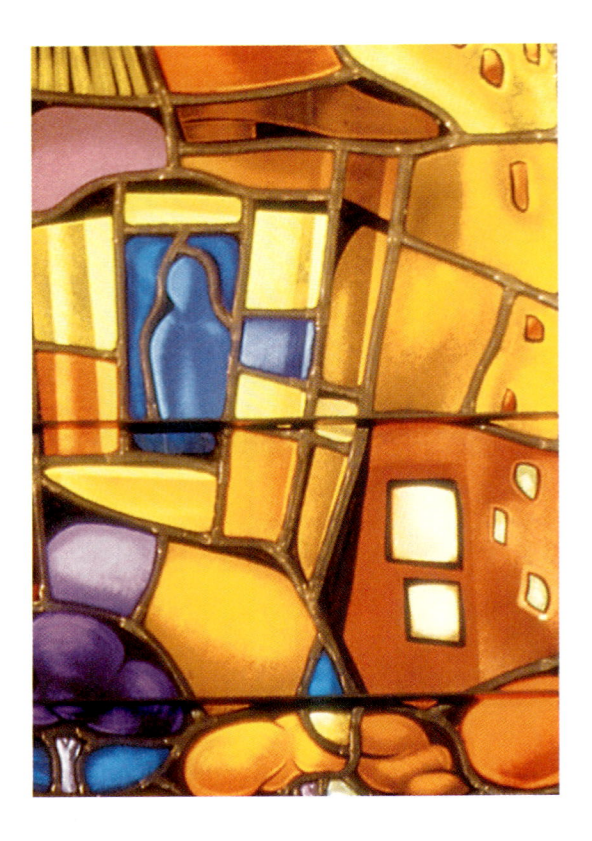

Broken Places

Looking forward from the cross, one could have seen the terraces of stone construction that were the city of Jerusalem in those days. Within the walls lived tens of thousands of Jews in what for them was the center of the universe, the holy city of God, Mt. Zion. The city held such hope, yet proved to be such a disappointment.

When Jesus first arrived from the north, he no doubt climbed to the top of the Mount of Olives and looked upon that great and beautiful city, full of promise, yet having lost its way. He wept and cried out,

O Jerusalem, Jerusalem!
killing the prophets and stoning those sent to you!
How often would I have gathered your children together
as a hen gathers her brood under her wings,
but you would not!
Behold, your house is desolate and forsaken.
— Matthew 23:37-38

Jesus lamented the plight of the city. But instead of raining down wrathful fire and destruction, Jesus gave his life, and call us beyond his life and death to work in the city, to go where people are, where suffering is, and to be the body of Christ in the city.

God knows we are not entirely able to do so. We are broken, we are flawed. But the cross has this miraculous power! Our brokenness, our wounds, can be used by God. If we are the body of Christ, then we are inevitably the broken body of Christ – but we need not despair. Ernest Hemingway once wrote that "the world breaks everyone, and then some become strong in the broken places." And Alan Jones said, "Everything has a crack in it. That's how the light gets in."

For beyond the cross there is light, and we are called to be that light, to be his body now on earth. A marvelous charter for the church is often attributed to Teresa of Avila:

Christ has no body now on earth but yours,
    no hands but yours,
    no feet but yours.
Yours are the eyes through which the compassion
    of Christ is to look out on a hurting world.
Yours are the feet with which he is to go about
    doing good.
Yours are the hands with which he is to bless now.

We work in the cities in which we find ourselves. We work in cities to which we are called, just as Paul heard that surprising call, "Come over to Macedonia and help us!" (Acts 16:9). If we listen and are attentive, God will call us into many places, to many people, as his body on earth now.

And we are liberated to follow because we know the truth about our eternal destiny with God. When John in the book of Revelation described our future existence with God, he painted it as a gleaming city, a new Jerusalem, as beautiful as a bride adorned for her wedding feast (Revelation 21:2). Words are inadequate to describe that new Jerusalem.

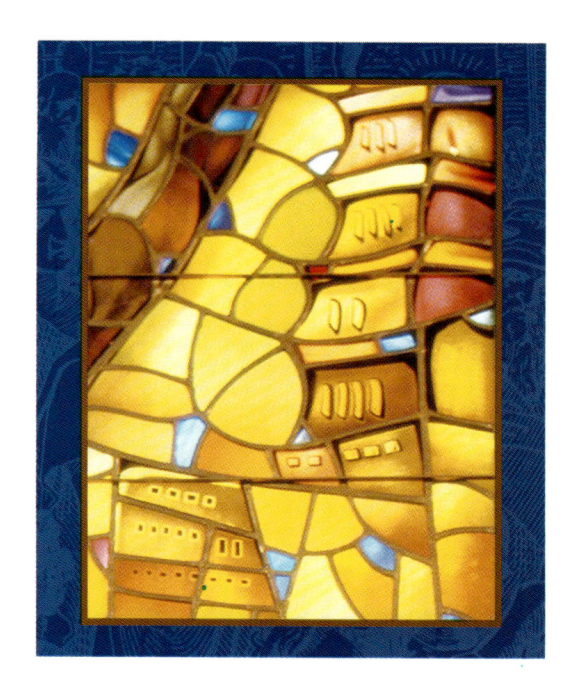

The city is built of pure gold, as clear as glass.
The foundations of the wall were adorned with every jewel.
The twelve gates were twelve pearls.
The street of the city was pure gold,
transparent as glass.

— REVELATION 21:18-21

C.S. Lewis was once asked if we could take this kind of description literally. His answer was that no, we should not take it literally – for the truth will be far greater than such words could ever express.

The Sower Went Out

Jesus told a story about a sower (Matthew 13:1-9). Some of his seed fell on the road, some among thorns, some in shallow soil – and did not flourish. But some seed fell into fertile soil, and produced a hundredfold.

In a way this story is a challenge to us, to be fertile, to let God's word take root in our souls. But moreso, it is a story about God. Jesus is saying that God is like that sower – flinging seed any and everywhere. When God gives away his grace, his love, he is not stingy, but incredibly generous, downright wasteful. God isn't just looking for people who are good bets to do well. God strews his love all over, in unlikely places, aggressive, hopeful, profligate.

A mystery is tucked away in a verse in the 15th chapter of Paul's first letter to the Corinthians. Unless a seed falls into the ground and dies, it cannot come to life; so it is with the resurrection. If you think about it, seeds grow in the dark. John Milton described life in our fallen world as "darkness visible." Being a seed in God's hand isn't all sweetness. We get sick, we suffer loss, we struggle with dysfunction – we are mortal. In the rose window, the sower's seeds fall at the foot of the cross. Jesus, the embodiment of God's love, died so we would never suffer or die alone. As his arms are spread on that cross, God's arms are casting seeds of hope into our darkness. God's arms enfold us in love.

For Easter is coming. When we think about our lives, we bet everything on Easter, on the too-good-not-to-be-true fact that the grave could not contain Jesus, that he lives, so that we might live, together, forever, with God, the seed having borne its ultimate fruit.

That life together we now call the Church. We think about Church using various metaphors, such as the image that we are the "body" of Christ. But another vivid image for what we're about is this sower, flinging seed any and everywhere. In the same way that God, in creating the world, would try anything, so we may try anything, not be skimpy, but profligate, eager to get the Gospel out to every place, to every person.

Not all of it is successful. Like Jesus' sower: some seed takes root, some doesn't. But if a lot of seed is flung around, surprises happen. We may make mistakes, and all is not lost because all belongs to God. Some mistakes are actually used by God for good. Even our human worst can be transformed into grace. In the remarkable little story in Genesis 37-45, Joseph's insanely jealous brothers sell him into slavery and convince their father that his favored son has been mauled by a wild animal.

But what an the this story has! God does not give them some kind of second chance, so they can rectify their errors are do better. On the contrary: God actually uses their foolishness, their sin, for God's good purposes (Genesis 45:1-8). If we serve such a God, then we can with reckless abandon fling what we have all over the place, knowing God is there through our resourceful and clever efforts, and also through our dimwitted, misguided efforts.

Lots of times, the success of something we do is not immediately obvious, or may be delayed for years. I know in my own life, I had a Sunday School teacher in the 5th grade, a coach in the 10th grade, a history professor as a freshman, a youth minister during college, even grandparents who died before I was grown up — all people who sowed seeds in me, who weeded and fertilized and watered my soul, and most of them never saw much result from what they did for me. But they changed me. We open our hands and take a meal to someone, teach a Sunday School class, drive a van, speak a word of hope, sit on a committee, place our offering in the plate, or smile — all just seeds, flung about. Seeds take time. We sow them, and trust God that as the rain comes down from heaven, and does not return without watering the earth, giving seed to the sower and bread to the eater, so shall my word be; it shall not return to me empty, but it will accomplish what I purpose (Isaiah 55:10-11).

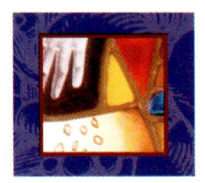

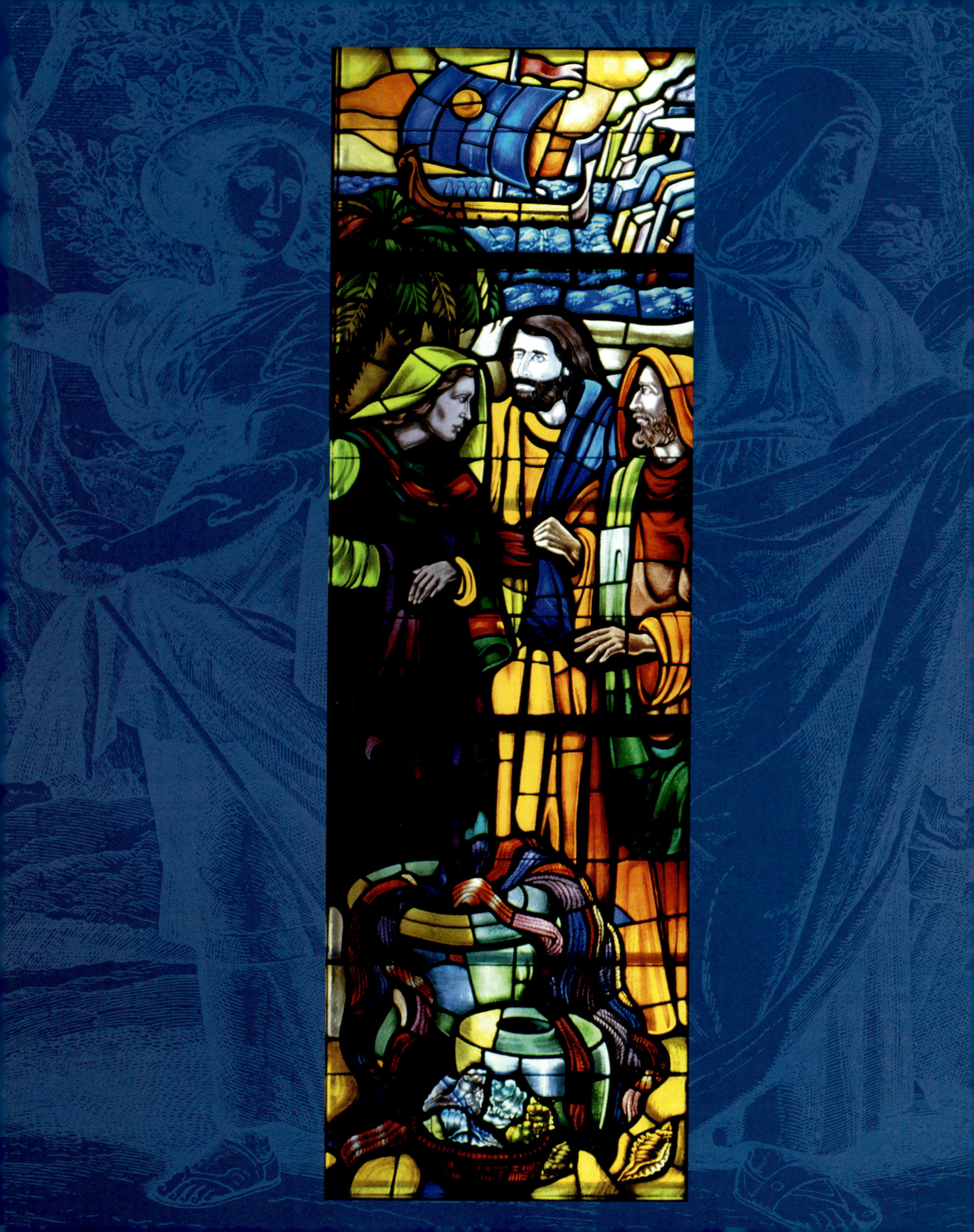

Lydia, Paul & Silas

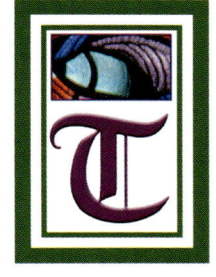

THE GREEK word which we translate "church" is ekklesia, which originally meant to be called (*klesia*) out (*ek*). The five windows on the west wall of the sanctuary appropriately look out onto Main Street, and symbolize how in our worship we too are called out into the world, to live out our faith out there, in the real world where God calls us to serve. While the first Christians were a small group in and around Jerusalem, they could not stay there, like a little club. Missionaries began to fan out all over the world, and no missionary had more zeal for reaching out to new people than Paul. In a day when roads were treacherous and mobility could be a crawl, Paul travelled all over Asia Minor (modern-day Turkey) until in a vision one night he heard the words, "Come over to Macedonia and help us!" That call (reported in Acts 16) meant taking the message of Christ to a new continent. But Paul did not hesitate. He and Silas boarded ship and sailed in just two days from Troas to Neapolis. Today this cruise would take a few hours. But in the ancient world, with the moodiness of the wind and the peril of a rocky seashore, such a trip would normally take a week or more! The swift trip was a clue that God had an urgency about getting the faith on over to Europe. Disembarking at Neapolis, Paul and Silas hiked up the road called Egnatia and came to Philippi.

On the Sabbath day, Paul searched for a synagogue. Finding none, they went down by the river, happened upon some women at prayer, and preached to them. The first convert was Lydia, a wealthy woman whose trade was in "purple goods," the color symbolic of affluence and even royalty. A native of Thyatira, back in Asia, she had settled into a lucrative business in Philippi. She had been a religious person, a regular worshipper of God. But even though she had a certain piety, she was surprised to find her life radically altered by the message Paul shared about this Jesus. For we are not called to be generally religious or spiritual, but rather to have a personal kind of relationship with the life, teaching, death and resurrection of this man, God made flesh, Jesus.

Acts 15 clarifies something crucial. Once she believed, and was baptized, she didn't just return to her home to resume business as usual. Rather, her home life was transformed. Immediately she offered hospitality to Paul and Silas. Later we learn that her home became the church in Philippi, as the earliest Christians had no sanctuaries, but met in the largest home available to them. Imagine her home, and imagine your home, transformed into a church, a center for doing ministry, reaching out to the poor, the lost, the hurting, those nobody else wants!

We know something about two of those who found a home in Lydia's house. A slave-girl, whose owners got rich by capitalizing on her phony soothsaying, was set free from her pagan bondage and set free to serve Christ. The owners, screaming that Paul and Silas were "disturbing our city," had the missionaries thrown in jail. But around midnight, they were singing hymns! During the Civil Rights movement, a preacher named James Bevel began singing "The Lord is my Shepherd." The jailer, thinking a radio was playing, so marvelous was Bevel's voice, rapped on the iron door, intending to confiscate the radio. Bevel responded, "You'll never take this radio away from me." The jailer then sat and listened, moved by his song. The jailer in Philippi too was moved by their joy, their faith. When an earthquake rattled the doors open, and the jailer almost took his life for fear he had lost his prisoners, we get a strange sense of who's free and who isn't. The jailer, holding the keys and the sword, isn't free at all. But the men behind those manmade bars are very much free, free to trust and praise God. Asking and receiving, the jailer believed in Christ, a move that no doubt cost him his job at the prison.

That's how it goes when we hear God's call to go out into the streets with our faith. Lives are changed, and not just the lives we manage to touch, but also our own. Slaves are freed. Jailers are freed. Houses become homes, spheres of hospitality, evidence of the love of Christ out in the world.

For the rest of his career, Paul enjoyed a warm relationship with his very close friends in Philippi. One of the treasures of the New Testament is his letter to them. He begins with a sparkling expression of thankfulness and love for them (Philippians 1:3-11). The epistle includes a beautiful hymn sung by the early Christians, which glorifies Christ Jesus who,

Though he was in the form of God,
did not count equality with God a thing to be grasped,
but emptied himself, taking the form of a servant, being born in the likeness of men.
And being found in human form he humbled himself,
and became obedient unto death,
even death on a cross.
Therefore God has highly exalted him,
and bestowed on him the name that is above every name,
that at the name of Jesus every knee should bow,
in heaven and on earth and under the earth,
and every tongue confess that
Jesus Christ is Lord,
to the glory of God the Father.
— Philippians 2:5-11

Paul's letter shimmers with joy and peace, all the more surprising since he wrote this letter from a jail cell. Paul knew that his ultimate citizenship was not in his home town of Tarsus, not in Damascus where he met Christ, not in Philippi where he had so many friends, but in heaven (3:20). And so whatever trials he faced, Paul wrote repeatedly, "Rejoice! Have no anxiety about anything. The peace of God, which passes all understanding, will keep your hearts and minds in Christ Jesus" (4:4-8).

*Rejoice! Have no anxiety about anything.
The peace of God, which passes all understanding,
will keep your hearts and minds in Christ Jesus.*

— St. Pa

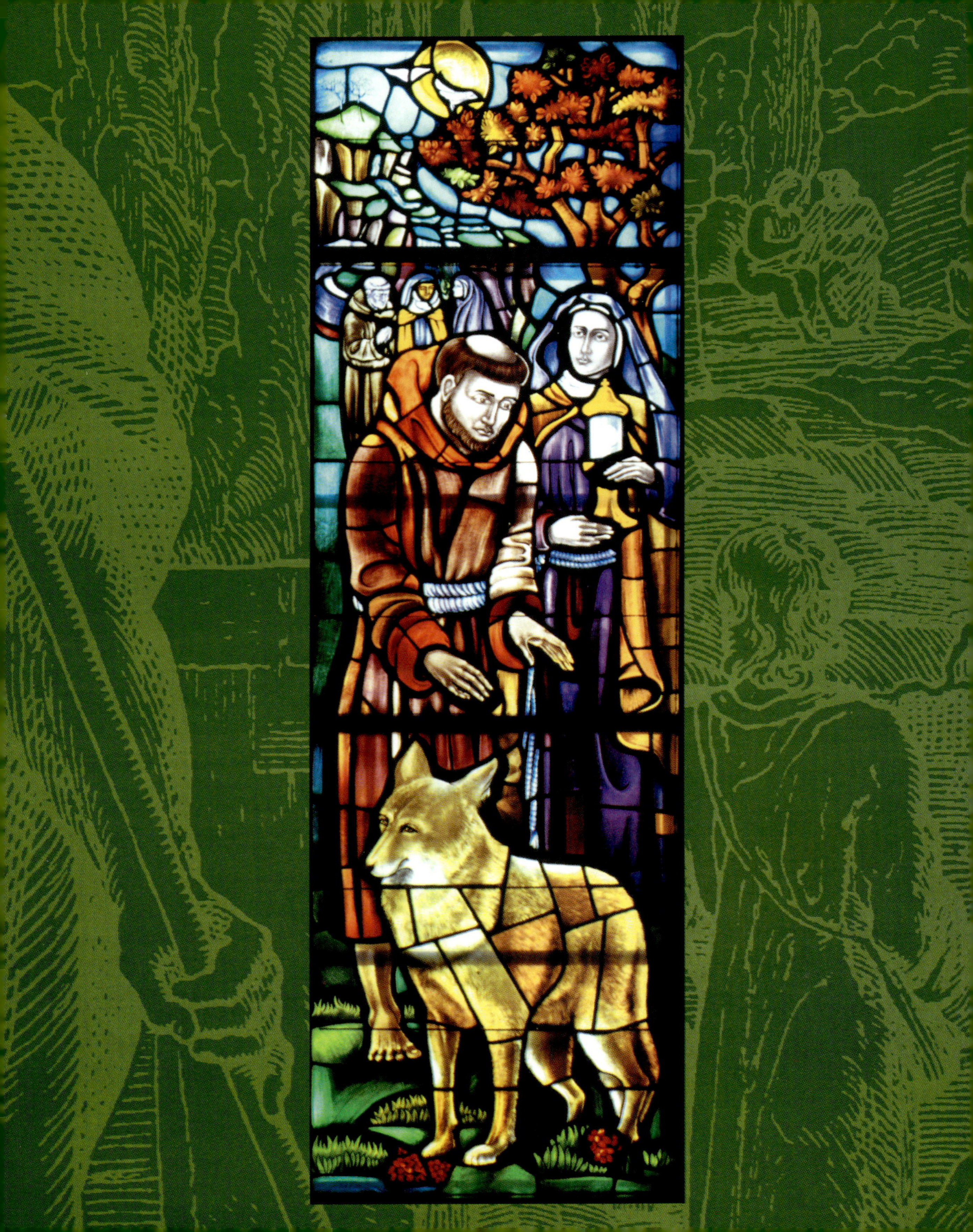

Clare & Francis of Assisi

JUST AS Lydia was in the business of trading exotic cloth, so was an upwardly mobile man from Italy of the twelfth century named Pietro Bernardone. The future of his son, Giovanni, was promising. The young man wore the latest fashions, sang like a troubadour, enjoyed immense popularity, and feigned a French accent – which is why they nicknamed him "frenchy" or "Francis."

God had other designs on this young man's life. As a young adult, he began to pray, so great was his anxiety over his life. One day, in an old crumbling church called San Damiano, Jesus, pictured on a byzantine crucifix, spoke to Francis: "Go, rebuild my church, for as you can see, it is falling into ruin." Francis began rebuilding San Damiano with his own hands, but the scope of his mission expanded until he was serving the poor and revolutionizing the church all over Europe.

When Pietro discovered that his son was literally giving away the family fortune in fabric, he locked him in a dungeon and took him to court. On trial, Francis stripped off his clothing, gave it back to his father, and said, "Until now I have called Pietro Bernardone my father. But from now on I will say 'Our father who art in heaven.'" Tragic in a way – but Jesus had warned that following after the kingdom of God may pit father against son.

Francis did not toss gold down over the city walls onto the poor outside. Rather, he lived among the poorest people, and wore the garments of the simplest peasant. G.K. Chesterton wrote that Francis "seemed to have liked everybody, but especially those whom everybody disliked him for liking." And again, "Francis had all his life a great liking for people who had been put hopelessly in the wrong." Lepers came to him. No physician would touch them – but Francis treated his "brothers in Christ" with tenderness, treating their wounds, embracing and kissing those who had been ostracized from society.

A rich man becoming poor! We may recall what Jesus said to the rich young ruler: "Sell all you have and give it to the poor" (Matthew 19:21). Francis had this naïve way of reading the Bible. He took it quite simply and literally – in the sense that he thought he was supposed to go out and do it.

Saints are those who challenge us to do what the Gospel is about, not just to think or talk about it. The very fact that this saint was rich, but was called to become poor, as was Lydia, may provide a clue for our society, with our bloated attachment to money and all it signifies. Our world measures personal worth and self-esteem by the ability to make money, and what money can purchase. Money seems to talk all day long. Money seems to be the fullness of life. Francis speaks gently to us across the centuries, and says that Christ alone is the fullness of life. Our worth and our self-esteem hinge only on the fact that we are made in God's image, that Jesus died for us, that we can be part of a community that loves as God loves.

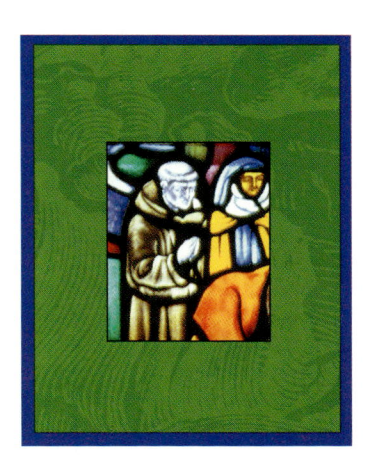

Famous for his tender friendships with animals, Francis taught us much about respecting and reveling in the wonders of nature, and also much about how to love those near to us, and those far from us. Once, Francis journeyed to the village of Gubbio. When he arrived, the city gates were bolted shut, the citizens armed with knives and fierce looks. A wolf had been terrorizing the village. He had actually devoured several of the citizens of Gubbio! When a posse would venture up into the hills, the wolf would hide, or manage to eat one of his hunters. Francis said, "I must pay a visit to my brother the wolf." The citizens offered him weapons, but he climbed up in the hills unarmed, the citizens atop the city wall anxiously watching for what they were sure would be the end of him.

Sure enough, the wolf appeared, snarling, drooling, baring his fangs. Just as he approached Francis, the saint pulled out a cross from his pocket. The wolf sat down. Francis spoke: "Brother wolf, I hear that you have been a great sinner, that you have terrorized this village and have even eaten its inhabitants. This is a great sin against God! If you repent, you may be forgiven." The wolf stared down toward the ground. Francis continued: "But I think I know why you've eaten the citizens of Gubbio. There is no food up in these hills. You are really just very hungry." The wolf looked up. Francis said, "I will make a deal with you. If you confess your sin, and promise not to terrorize these people any longer, I will get them to feed you every day." Francis reached down, and the wolf offered his paw in return.

At first the citizens of Gubbio were suspicious, on their guard. But after a time they began to trust the wolf. Brother wolf came in and out of their homes at his leisure. He was like a pet to them. Two years later, when he died, the citizens of Gubbio wept for days. And in 1873, workers raised a flagstone and uncovered a wolf's skull, elaborately buried beneath a chapel dedicated to St. Francis. Carlo Carretto wisely concluded, "The miracle of the story is not that the wolf became tame. Rather, the miracle is that the citizens of Gubbio became tame."

Francis understood and handled with care the sanctity of God's world. One of his poetic prayers began, "All praise be yours, my Lord, through all that you have made," and went on to speak of "my brother the sun, who brings the day, and the light you give us through him," and then of "my sister the moon, so bright, precious and fair." Once he was out walking and looked up into the trees, in whose branches were countless birds. He preached to them: "*O birds, my sisters, you must praise God always, for he has given you freedom to fly, and the gift of the wind and air. You neither sow nor reap, yet*

God feeds you, giving you streams to drink from, and trees in which you can build your nests. You neither sow nor spin, yet God clothes you and your children. The Creator loves you dearly, and so beware of the sin of ingratitude, and be always eager to praise God." Perhaps we too may notice our brothers and sisters in creation, and be grateful.

Francis was not alone for long in his craziness. Bernardo of Quintavalle, a wealthy merchant, invited Francis to his home. After the evening meal, they retired for the evening. Francis pretended to sleep; Bernard also pretended to sleep, even feigning a snore. Francis rose and then knelt, praying over and over, all night long, "My God, my all." Bernard was touched, and asked Francis in the morning how to become a servant of God. Bernard too became poor, as did other young men, Giles, Masseo, Leo, and hundreds more. So alarmed were the fathers of the city that they quarantined the young men, fearing (rightly!) that some strange sort of contagion had broken loose.

The greatest servant among them may have been Brother Juniper. So serious was Juniper about imitating Christ that he would give away the very clothes off his back. After several embarrassing episodes, Juniper's superior ordered him not to give his tunic, or any part of it, to a beggar. But soon Juniper was approached by a pauper asking for alms. He replied, "I have nothing to give, except this tunic, and I cannot give it to you due to my vow of obedience. However, if you steal it from me, I will not stop you." Left naked, Juniper returned to the other friars and told them he had been robbed. His compassion became so great that he gave away, not only his own things, but the books, altar linens, and capes belonging to other friars. When the poor came to brother Juniper, the other friars would hide their belongings so he could not find them.

The adventure of Francis included women, especially Clare. Younger than Francis, she loved and admired him, and became the epitome of holiness and charity, founding the resilient order of the Poor Clares. Immediately after her death, the Catholic church canonized her. One testimonial in her dossier read, "Her very life was for others a school of instruction and doctrine. In this book of life others learned the rule of life; in this mirror of life others beheld the path of their own life."

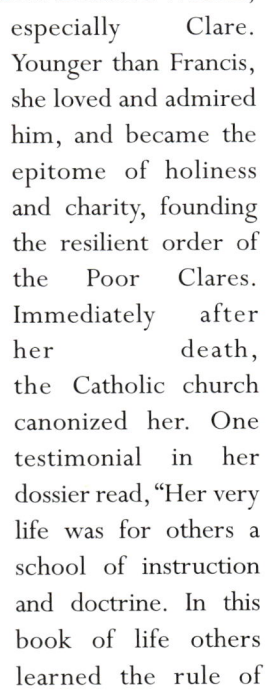

Francis and Clare, in their lives of good humor and great joy, remind us that we are called to be "fools" for Christ, not to work so hard to "fit in" to a culture out of sync with Christ. They invite us to be a little more reckless, a little more passionate, about doing what's in the Bible, about serving the poor, about loving Christ. On the night of October 3, 1226, Francis died. His last words were "I have done what is mine to do. Now it is yours to do what is yours to do."

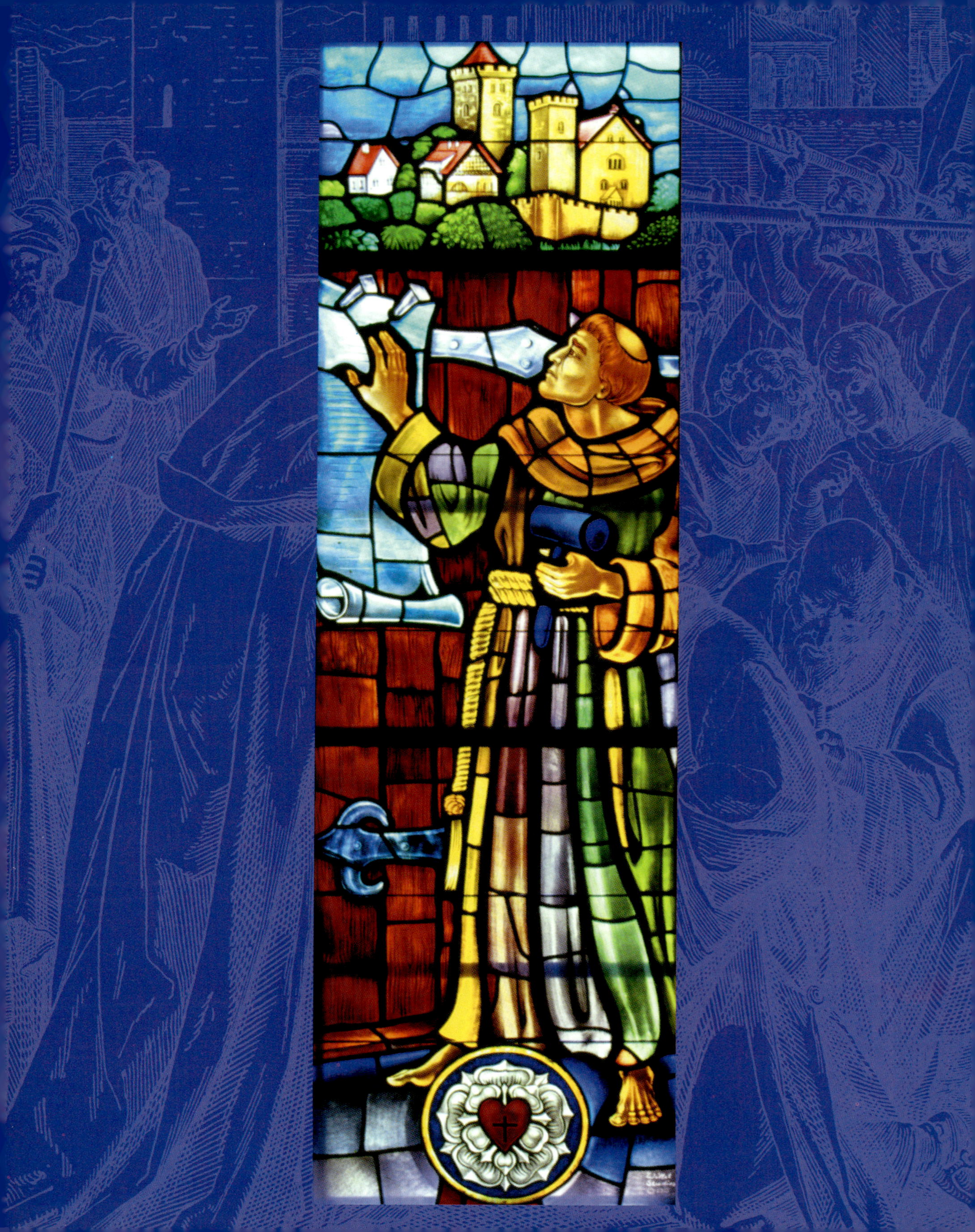

Martin Luther

AT HIGH noon on October 31, 1517, an obscure professor of Old Testament nailed ninety-five theses to the door of the parish church in Wittenberg, Germany. The firestorm that ensued provoked Pope Leo to complain, "A wild boar has invaded my vineyard."

Luther grew up in a humble, quiet home. At first he wished to become a lawyer. But he was struck to the ground during a thunderstorm when he was 21, and vowed to become a monk should he survive. His zealous pursuit of the religious life staggers the mind. Regimented prayers, frequent fasting, coarse clothing, and mortification of the body were more than just his daily routine. He was trying to reach God, to escape his sinful nature, to be good enough to be a part of God's kingdom.

Fortunately for us, Luther's job was teaching the Bible, which forced him to keep reading, and thinking, and reading more in that Bible. What he kept hearing from that Bible, and the way it clashed with current church practice, drove him to nail those theses on the Wittenberg door, and to dare to offend the emperor, who was gouging the poor to build the massive basilica of St. Peter's in Rome. Luther declared, "We should rear living temples, …and last of all St. Peters." "The pope would do better to sell St. Peter's and give the money to the poor folk who are being fleeced by the hawkers of indulgences."

Summoned to stand trial before the Diet of Worms, Luther was shown a pile of his books: "Are these yours?" "They are all mine," he proudly claimed, and then characteristically added, "and I have written more." To the demand that he repudiate his books, and all he was preaching and teaching, Luther boldly stood up to the arrayed might of the Holy Roman Empire and the pope's legates: "My conscience is captive to the Word of God. I cannot and I will not recant anything, for to go against conscience is neither right nor safe. Here I stand, I cannot do otherwise. God help me."

Somehow Luther stayed just out of harm's way, and lived for 25 more years, in which he translated the Bible into German, so regular folks could read and understand. Luther produced catechisms, focusing on the Apostles' Creed, the Lord's Prayer, and the Ten Commandments, so families could participate in religious education. Parents were to inquire into their children's souls and discipleship week by week, and were urged to withhold food from children who were less than zealous for the cause! Worship was transformed, for Luther insisted that the congregation be involved in worship, which is not a show by the priests, but our common offering to God. For Luther, there was nothing like a good hymn to drive away the devil! Luther had encouraged the usage of hymns

Luther's personal "seal" incorporated a cross, symbolic of Christ; a heart, symbol of our faith; a white rose as an image of joy, consolation and peace; and a golden ring, emblematic of the endless bliss of heaven.

in the vernacular, and wrote a few himself, most famously "A Mighty Fortress," written at a time of profound depression in his own life. He wrote, "Music is a fair and lovely gift of God which has often wakened and moved me to the joy of preaching ... I have no use for cranks who despise music, because it is a gift of God. Music drives away the devil and makes people gay; they forget thereby all wrath, unchastity, arrogance and the like. Next after theology I give to music the highest place and the greatest honor..."

Luther helped us understand freedom. We may feel free, but we are not. I can decide to stand here or there, to do this or that — but all my supposedly free movements happen behind bars. I am very much trapped by sin, as if I have tumbled into a tangle of barbed wire, from which I absolutely cannot extricate myself. I am not free to decide for or against God. It is only the unmerited grace of God that sets me free. Righteousness isn't my impeccable holiness, but rather a gift God freely bestows on us. What needs to be altered is not this or that behavior, but rather the whole of human nature. Justification is waking up to realize that we have been set into a right relationship with God, through no doing of our own. Our receiving of this free gift we call "faith."

But the gift is all gift, and it is unveiled in the cross of Christ. Luther thought often of the lowliness of Mary, that there was no room at the inn, observing that God made himself small for us in Christ, showing us his heart, so that our hearts might be won. We do not need to ascend to God; God has descended to us. God came as a child, all gentleness, tenderness; no one need be afraid of a child. On Palm Sunday, Jesus entered Jerusalem as a king. But he left all the pomp, castles, and gold to other kings. They enter cities on purebred stallions, accompanied by an impressive entourage; but Jesus is poor and wretched, riding on a donkey as a poor beggar-king.

God is most fully made known, not in some obvious victory, but in the apparently contradictory moment of the crucifixion. It is when God hides himself, when God is absent, when all is darkness, in the middle of suffering, that God is genuinely present, embracing our mortality and suffering. In the ninety-five theses, Luther stated, "God works by contraries so that a man feels himself to be lost in the very moment when he is on the point of being saved. Man must first cry out that there is no health in him. In this disturbance salvation begins. When a man believes himself to be utterly lost, light breaks."

When he died in 1546, many people feared his reformation would end. But the movement was not his, nor anyone else's. It depended on the power and creativity of God, and once the word of God was unleashed there was no reining it back in. The church always, in every age and in every place, including right here, stands in need of reform. We are never fully the church God calls us to be.

Back in 1978, another great church reformer, Archbishop Oscar Romero, preached a sermon about the church's sacred but difficult task:

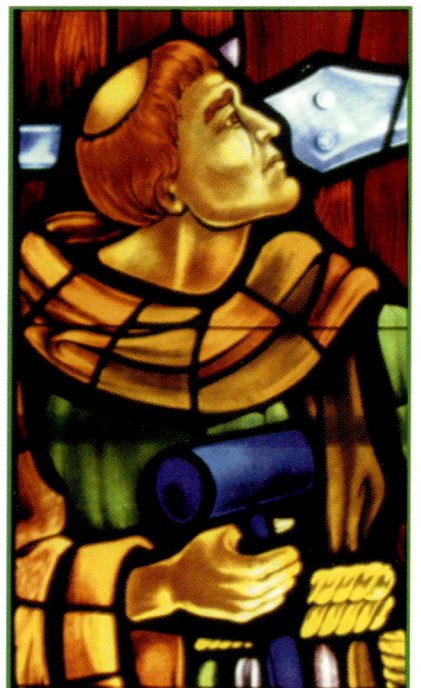

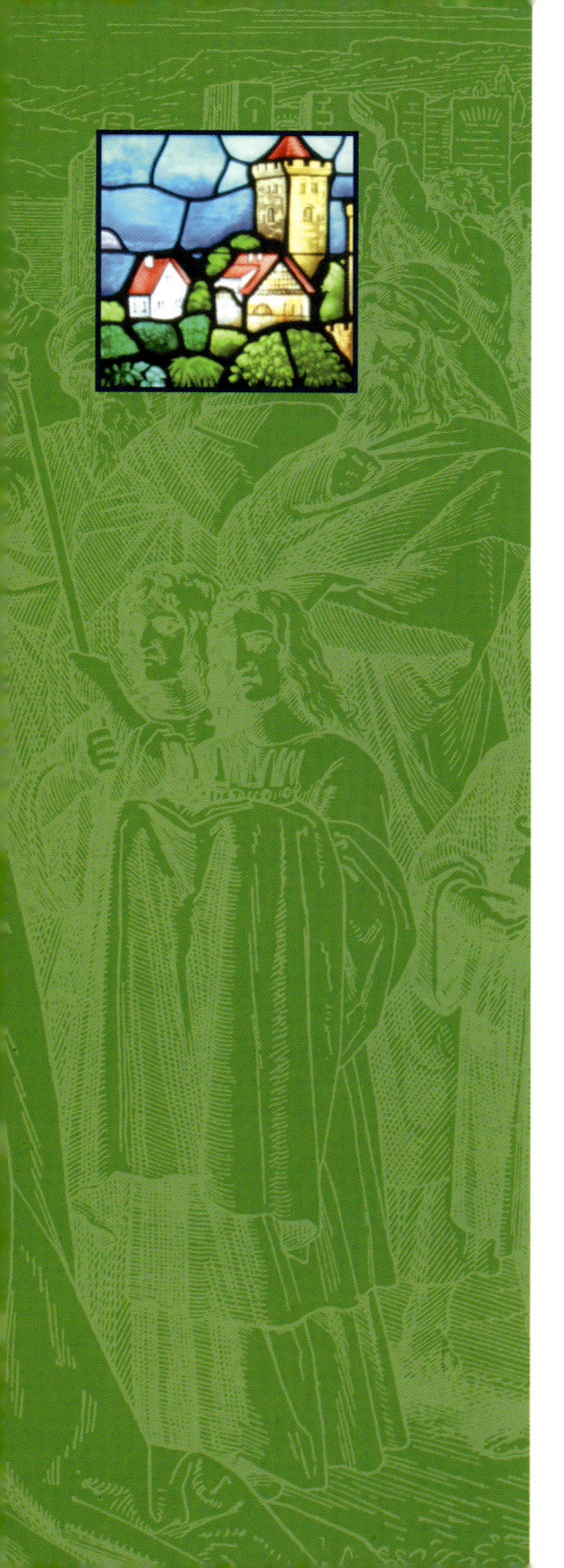

*This is the mission entrusted to the church,
    a hard mission:
to uproot sins from history,
to uproot sins from the political order,
to uproot sins from the economy,
to uproot sins where they are.
    What a hard task!
It has to meet conflicts amid so much selfishness,
so much pride,
so much vanity,
so many who have enthroned the reign of sin among us.
The church must suffer for speaking the truth,
    for pointing out sin,
    for uprooting sin.
No one wants to have a sore spot touched,
and therefore a society with so many sores twitches
when someone has the courage to touch it
and say 'You have to treat that.
    You have to get rid of that.
    Believe in Christ.
    Be converted.'*

Thank God for reformers like Luther and Romero, and Francis, and Wesley, and many others God has raised up, for their courage, their willingness to touch the sore spots, their healing touch. We are healed as people and as a church when we are converted, when we let the Bible correct our vision, when we believe in Christ.

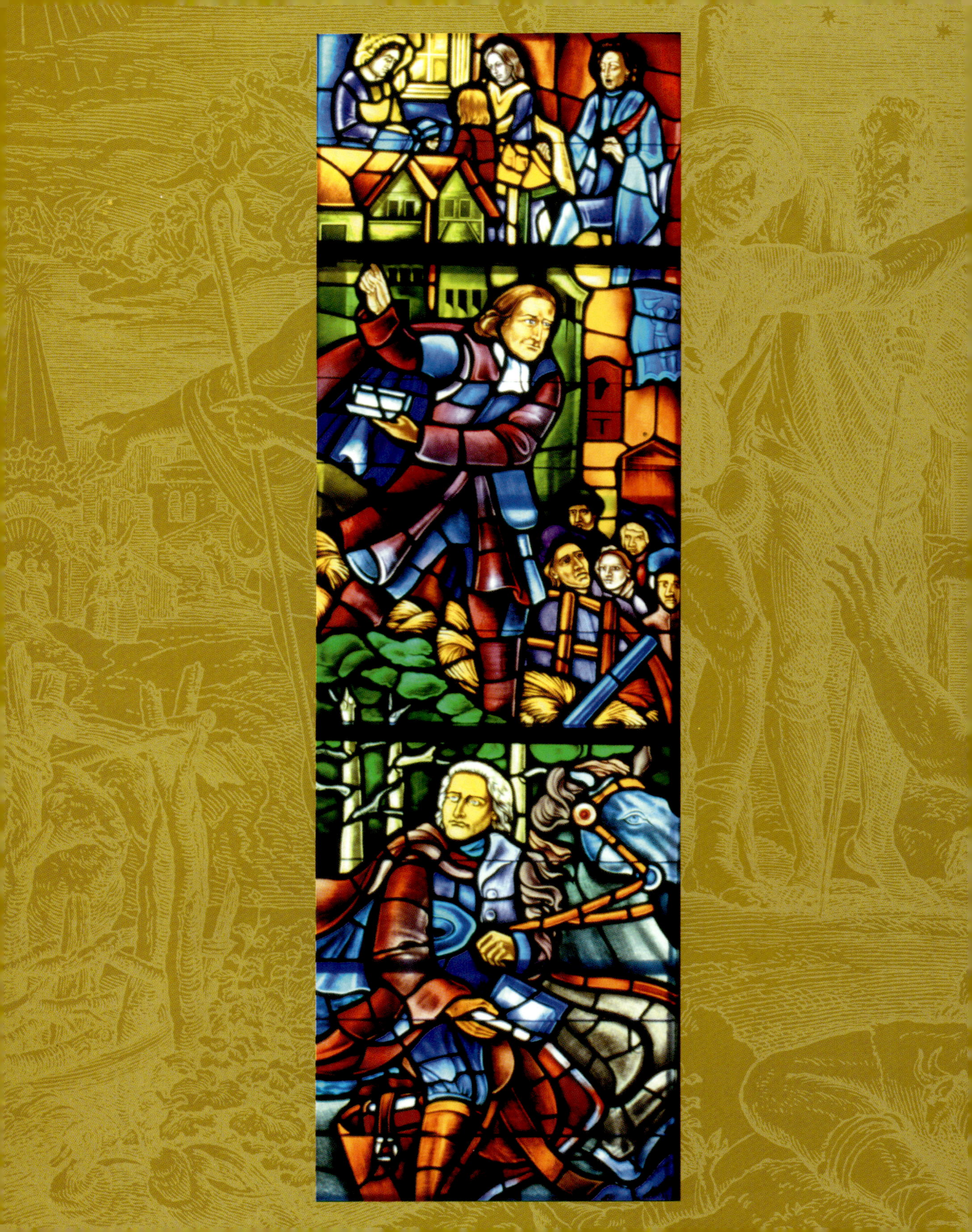

John Wesley & Francis Asbury

IN 1697, Samuel Wesley became the rector of the Anglican church in Epworth. His wife, Susannah, bore him nineteen children, the fifteenth being named John, born June 17, 1703. He was called "Jacky" by his mother, and she admitted to being "more particularly careful of the soul of this child," probably because of one cold winter night in 1709. The thatched roof of the parsonage caught on fire. Scrambling outside as the house was engulfed in flames, the family counted heads — and one was missing, five-year-old John. His father was kneeling in prayer, commending the child's soul to heaven, when three neighbors climbed on each other's shoulders and rescued little Jacky through a window. They forever called him "a brand plucked out of the burning," and figured he had some special God-given task to fulfill.

He learned that task at his mother's knee. She was rigorous in the education of her many children, as their home was structured on discipline, prayer, Bible study, and hymn-singing. Among her prayers were these words:

Help me, Lord, to remember that religion is not to be confined to the church, or closet, nor exercised only in prayer and meditation, but that everywhere I am in thy presence. So may my every word and action have a moral content. May all the happenings of my life prove useful and beneficial to me. May all things instruct me and afford me an opportunity of exercising some virtue and daily learning and growing toward thy likeness... Amen.

The genius of John Wesley was that his religion was most certainly not confined to the church. Methodists think often of that night in May, 1738, when his heart was "strangely warmed." He had nearly died on a ship returning to England from Savannah, Georgia — and was thunderstruck by the calm and faith of the Moravians on board, who sang calmly, joyfully in the face of imminent disaster. He wanted, and got, that faith for himself.

But what is so fascinating about Wesley is not that he had a profound experience of the grace of God one night. Rather, it was what he did by day, day after day, taking the Gospel out into the streets. Literally: instead of just preaching in gilded sanctuaries where the religious folks were, he went out to the coal-miners, to the prisons, anywhere he could find people who might listen. So fiery was his preaching, so provocative was the message of the Gospel, that riots broke out.

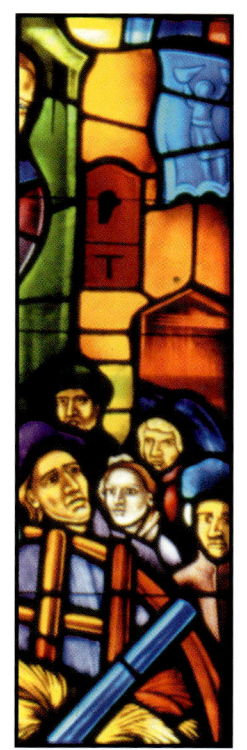

John Wesley not only preached, but he was a "doer of the Word" (James 1:22). He campaigned for the rights of orphans forced to labor in sweat shops. He educated the penniless, fed the hungry, struggled against social and economic injustice. His legacy to us Methodists is this marvelous blending of personal devotion to Christ and zealous service out in the world. We are most Methodist when we cultivate a deep relationship with God and live it out by serving the needy.

We are also most Methodist when we do it together. Wesley insisted that all Methodists be part of a "class," what we might call a small group, more akin to Alcoholics Anonymous than anything else. The people were to have "a desire to flee from the wrath to come," and to give "evidence of their desire for salvation." They would meet together each week for prayer, study and song. But then they would speak "freely and plainly the true state of our souls," and would confess faults and sins, being probingly questioned by others in the group, holding each other accountable, knowing how desperately we need each other to grow in faith and holiness.

At age 83, Wesley voiced a haunting prophecy: "I am not afraid that the people called Methodists should ever cease to exist either in Europe or America. But I am afraid, lest they should only exist as a dead sect, having the form of religion without the power." Wesley surely knew the power. On his deathbed in 1791, with a handful of friends gathered to wait and watch, John Wesley surprised everyone by breaking a long silence with a song (which was a hymn by Isaac Watts):

> *I'll praise my Maker while I've breath,*
> *and when my soul is lost in death,*
> *praise shall employ my nobler powers.*
> *My days of praise shall ne'er be past...*

Singing praises to God came naturally to the Wesley family, given Susannah's inclinations. John's brother Charles wrote an astounding 6,500 hymns before his death in 1788, averaging a hymn each day of his adult life! His hymns were "not the product of a lively imagination...nor were they the fruit of hard mental toil. They were the spontaneous effusions of his heart." From that heart we have learned to think of Jesus as "lover of my soul," to harken to "the herald angels" at Christmas, to long to have the absurdly high number of "a thousand tongues to sing my great redeemer's praise." This latter hymn stands as the first in virtually every collection of Methodist hymns. On the day of Pentecost in 1738, Charles attended a Moravian service, and at midnight gave his life to Christ — less than a week before his brother John's more famous Aldersgate experience of the "heart strangely warmed." "O For a Thousand Tongues" was written to commemorate that conversion. Stretching to 18 stanzas, the image wasn't entirely original; his mentor, Peter Bühler, had written, "Had I a thousand tongues, I would praise him with them all!"

Wesley's goal was "to arouse sinners, encourage saints, and to educate all in the mysteries of the Christian faith." Charles Wesley understood that hymns were not just inspirational, but also educational. He used contemporary folks tunes, melodies from Italian opera, as well as oratorio (especially favoring Handel). It was by the singing of hymns that the early Methodists learned theology, were reshaped as people of faith, and catapulted into the streets in mission.

As a young man, John Wesley tried his hand at preaching in America, spending months in Oglethorpe's colony in Savannah. The enduring beginnings of Methodism in this country can be attributed to Francis Asbury, one of the first bishops of a new denomination begun in 1784.

*"Whither am I going?
To the New World.
What to do?
To gain Honour? No.
To get money? No.
I am going to live for God,
and to bring others to do so.
The people God owns
are the Methodists.
The doctrines we preach,
the discipline we enforce are,
I believe, the purest of any
people in the world."*

— FRANCIS ASBURY,
EMBARKING FOR AMERICA, 1771

Wesley did not wish to break off from the Church of England, but the rancor of the Revolutionary War left him little choice. Francis Asbury was no regal bishop in an ivory tower. He came to America in 1771, and from that moment until his death in 1816 he never owned a home, and he never even rented a room. He lived literally on the road and slept wherever he was, in the cabins of settlers, or on the ground out in the woods. He rode on horseback an estimated 228,000 miles, up and down the east coast, across the Alleghenies, and throughout North Carolina, preaching in Lincolnton, Terrell, Sugar Creek, Mocksville, Pineville, planting little bands of Methodists who eventually gave birth to dozens of churches in our region, such as our own. In those days, revivals and camp meetings were the social events of the year. The Rock Springs Camp Ground in Denver was established in 1797 and still runs each summer.

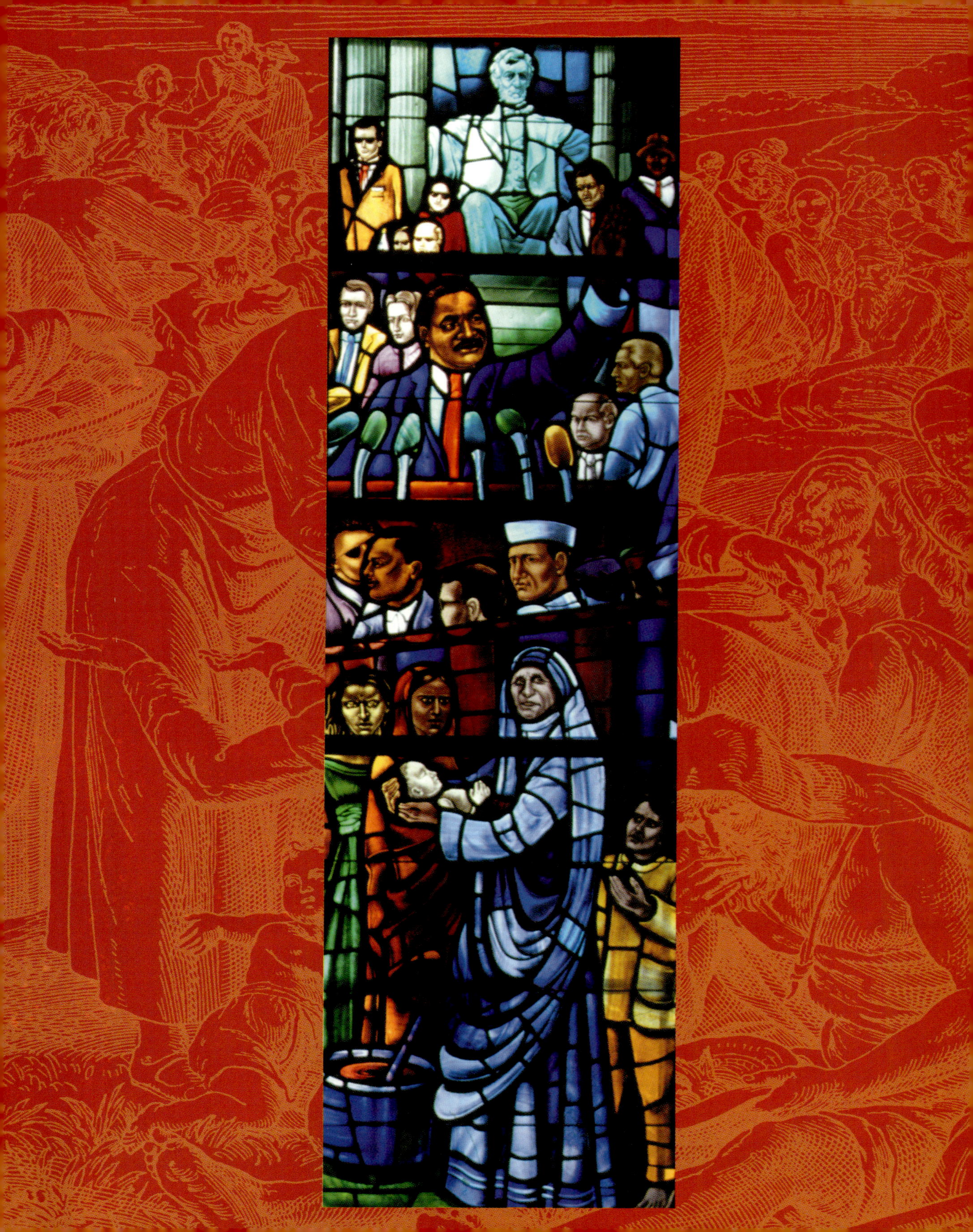

Mother Teresa & Martin Luther King

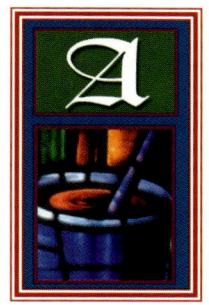

AS WE are called out as the church into service in Christ's name, we need to remember that the great heroes of the faith were not just once-upon-a-very-long-time-ago characters sleeping safely in some museum. They live in our own lifetimes, in our own part of the world, perhaps even in our own town, maybe in our own homes.

I took my daughter to see Mother Teresa in the Charlotte coliseum. When the venerable old servant of the poor walked on stage, and the tumultuous applause finally died down, my daughter said, "Daddy, she looks like somebody in the Bible." Indeed, she did. Her whole life was about taking the teachings of Jesus very seriously, and putting them into practice.

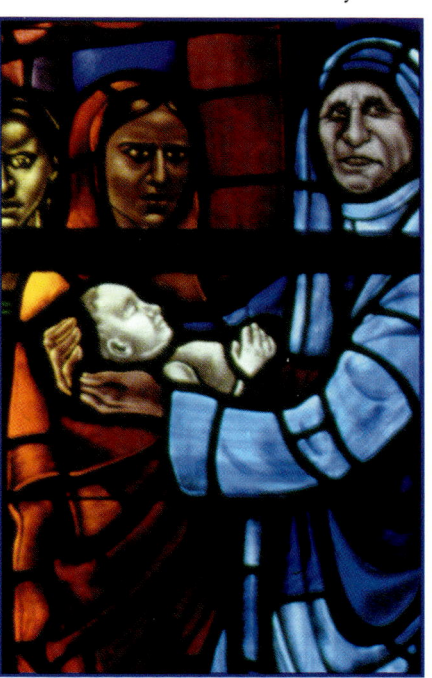

Mother Teresa's life was an embodied sermon on Matthew 25:31-46, Jesus' last lesson which was for her both a blueprint for action and a source of joy. "The Missionaries of Charity do firmly believe that they are touching the body of Christ in his distressing disguise whenever they are helping and touching the poor. We cannot do this with a long face." For Mother Teresa, service was not somehow the outcome of prayer, or something done when not praying. Serving the poor, and opening the heart to Christ, were one and the same. She taught the sisters "to pray while working, doing it for Jesus and doing it to Jesus. This brings a tremendous closeness with him."

In 1946, on the train to Darjeeling, she heard a voice, calling her to reach out to the poorest of the poor. Her mission was to find food and medicine, but mostly it was to love. Thousands, quite literally, could be counted as "failures": they died while she was with them. But her mission was to love, to lend to strangers the greatest of all dignities, that you need not die alone. One by one she picked up thousands of the destitute and suffering.

One by one she took other young women by the hand and set them to picking up the destitute and suffering. Girls she had taught began to follow her into the streets — and for many, the work meant descending many notches in the Indian caste system. Once a wealthy Hindu woman came, offering aid. During the conversation, she admitted how much she loved beautiful saris; in fact, she spent 800 rupees each month on a new sari. Mother Teresa, whose distinctive white cotton sari with a blue stripe cost eight rupees, thought this the place to begin. "Next time, when you go to buy a sari, instead of buying a sari for 800 rupees, you buy a sari worth 500 rupees and with the remaining 300 you buy saris for the poor people." More than the shifting of money was at stake; the elegance of a sari was a symbol of a woman's status, her notch in the caste system. But the woman did it, and over time came down to paying just 100 rupees for her sari, giving the rest away. Teresa urged her, "Please do not go below 100!" The woman reported that her life was transformed, that she received far more than she ever gave.

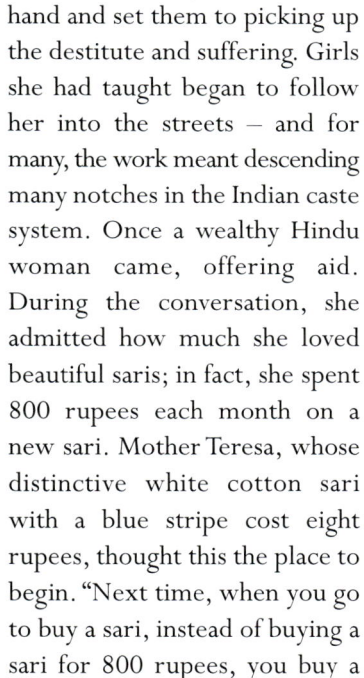

Once a wealthy western woman visited Mother Teresa in Calcutta, and offered to write a check to support the work of the Sisters of Charity. Mother declined: "I won't take your money." The woman insisted, reminding this human roadblock that she had great resources. But Mother still said "No money." Exasperated, the woman stammered, "Well what can I do?" Mother said, "Come and see." She led the woman by the hand down into a dreadful barrio, found a desperately dirty, hungry child, and asked the woman to take care of him. Her pocketbook being of no avail, the woman took a cloth and water basin and bathed the child. Then she spooned cereal into the child's mouth. She reported later that her life was changed. Mother Teresa told us all the truth:

> At the end of life we will not be judged by
> how many diplomas we have received,
> how much money we have made,
> how many great things we have done.
> We will be judged by,
> I was hungry and you gave me to eat,
> I was naked and you clothed me,
> I was homeless and you took me in.

An atheist watched one such servant as she went about her business. Later he claimed that he had seen Jesus for the first time in his life — and in Calcutta, of all places.

Another great saint of the twentieth century, Dorothy Day, suggested there is another dimension to holiness and service in our world.

> "Whatever I had read as a child about the saints had thrilled me. I could see the nobility of giving one's life for the sick, the maimed, the leper. But why was so much done in remedying the evil instead of avoiding it in the first place? Where were the saints to try to change the social order, not just to minister to the slaves, but to do away with slavery?"

Martin Luther King, Jr., was called by God to change the social order, to lead us to a new way of being, or rather, to remind us how God made the world and intended us to exist all along. His famous speech on the steps of the Lincoln Memorial in August of 1963 was not just his vision, but rather God's vision for humanity, and an ongoing challenge for every community and church:

> *I still have a dream... that one day this nation will rise up and live out the true meaning of its creed — that all men are created equal. I have a dream that one day on the red hills of Georgia, sons of former slaves and sons of former slave-owners will be able to sit down together at the table of brotherhood. I have a dream my four little children will one day live in a nation where they will not be judged by the color of their skin but by the contents of their character. I have a dream that one day, down in Alabama, little black boys and black girls will join hands with little white boys and little white girls as sisters and brothers. Then we will be able to speed up that day when all of God's children, black men and white men, Jews and Gentiles, Catholics and Protestants, will be able to join hands and sing in the words of the old Negro spiritual, 'Free at last, free at last, thank God almighty, we are free at last.'*

Lincoln, looming in marble behind Dr. King, had spoken in his second inaugural, just days before his death, of "malice toward none, with charity for all, let us strive on to finish the work we are in, to bind up the nation's wounds." Such still is our call.

Lincoln himself, not a great church-goer, noted at Gettysburg how the deaths of others consecrated the ground on which they stood, and it is because

> 'Free at last,
> free at last,
> thank God
> almighty, we
> are free at last.'

of those others that we dedicate ourselves to their unfinished work, "that from these honored dead we take increased devotion." These windows are memorials to women and men like Teresa and Lydia, Wesley and Luther, Clare and Paul, and Jesus himself, who most certainly did not die in vain. These windows are also dedicated in honor and in memory of women and men who have consecrated our world, and our church, by their lives. That they have been here, and have taken their faith out there, and with them into their eternal destiny, is our mandate to increased devotion, as the life of God, and our life with God, take on shape, and color, and light.

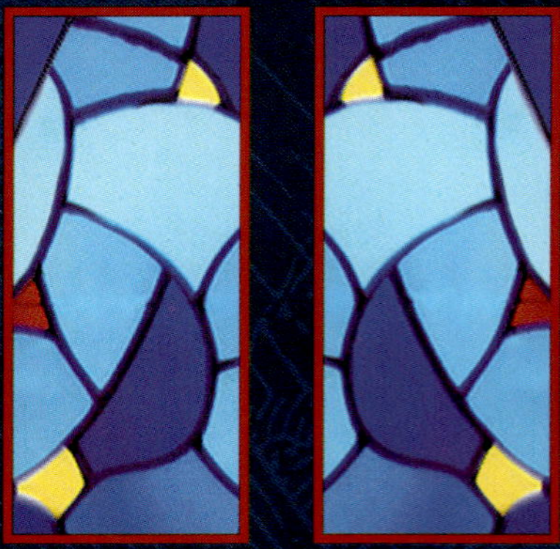

Light of the World

Finally we come to a window on the west, toward the sunset, a radiant burst of light. God's first action reported in the Bible is stunning in its simplicity.

> *God said, "Let there be light."*
> *And there was light.*
> *God saw that the light was good.*
> *And God separated the light from the darkness.*
> — Genesis 1:3-4

We might have preferred that God simply banished the darkness. We urge children not to be afraid of the dark. But there is plenty of darkness in our world. Suffering of every kind, sin, hollowness, depression (which William Styron called "darkness visible"). Dorothy Sayers, the great mystery writer, composed the following scene in *The Devil to Pay*. Speaking to the devil, Faustus asks, "Who made thee?" His answer:

MEPHISTOPHELES: *God; as the light makes the shadow.*
FAUSTUS: *Is God, then, evil?*
MEPHISTOPHELES: *God is only light,*
  And in the heart of the light no shadow standeth,
  Nor can I dwell within the light of heaven
  Where God is all.
FAUSTUS: *What art thou, Mephistopheles?*
MEPHISTOPHELES: *I am the price that all things pay*
   for being,
  The shadow on the world, thrown by the world
  Smiling in its own light, which light God is

God does not cause suffering, is not the author of evil. God is light, and sheds light on our lives and our world. The precious gift of the Bible:

> *Thy word is a lamp to my feet*
> *and a light to my path.*
> — Psalm 119:105

Even the stars. Somehow in God's intergalactic designs a star of unusual brilliance settled over the small, hardly noticeable town of Bethlehem. Magi, men of wisdom who searched the night skies for clues to the meaning of the universe, tracked that star and found the secret of life in a stable. Barbara Brown Taylor preached a sermon in which she imagined the angels and God discussing how best to rescue a wayward world. At length God suggested he create himself as a baby. At first the archangels were silent, but then they tried to talk God out of such a foolish plan. They would worry, for he would be putting himself at the mercy of wayward creatures. No security in such a plan. But God decided to take the risk. He was willing to risk everything to get as close as possible to his creatures, in hopes they might love him again.

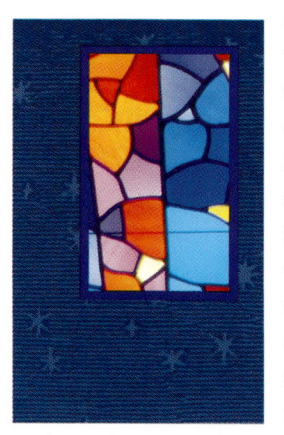

"It was a daring plan, but once the angels saw that God was dead set on it, they broke into applause – not the uproarious kind but the steady kind that goes on and on when you have witnessed something you know you will never see again. While they were still clapping, God turned around the left and chamber, shedding his robes as he went. The angels watched as his midnight blue mantle fell to the floor, so that all the stars on it collapsed in a heap. Then a strange thing happened. Where the robes had fallen, the floor melted and opened up to reveal a scrubby brown pasture speckled with sheep and a bunch of shepherds sitting around drinking wine. It was hard to say who was more startled, the shepherds or the angels. Looking down at the human beings who were trying to hide behind each other, one angel said in as gentle a voice as he could muster, 'Do not be afraid, for I am bringing you good news of great joy for all the people: to you is born this day in the city of David a savior, who is the Messiah, the Lord.' And away up the hill, from the direction of town, came the sound of a newborn baby's cry."

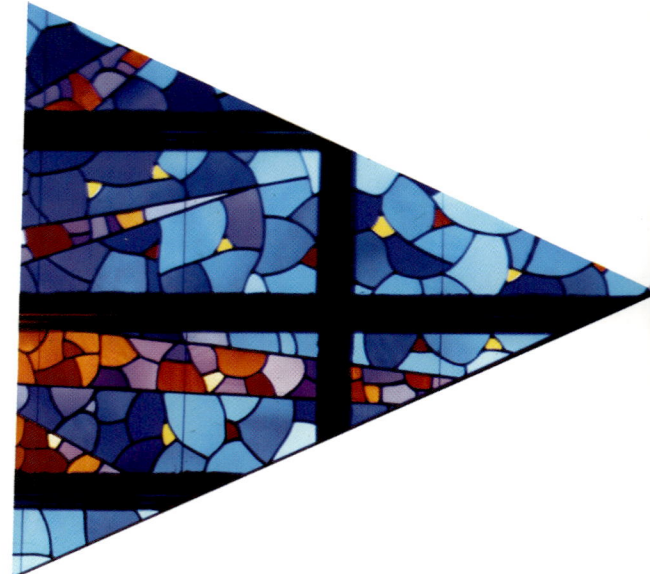

That baby grew up, and his favorite miracle seemed to be curing blind people. For Jesus was all about banishing darkness. He told them, and us:

> *I am the light of the world.*
> *He who follows me will not walk in darkness,*
> *but will have the light of life.*
> — JOHN 8:12

And what are Christ's followers supposed to be?

> *You are the light of the world.*
> *Let your light so shine before others,*
> *that they may see your good works*
> *and give glory to your Father who is in heaven.*
> — MATTHEW 5:14, 16

We are light, for God is light. We reflect the splendor of God's light — perhaps even in the midst of our inability and failures. Scott Peck spoke of how "friction" can be good for a relationship. Friction produces heat, which may make us want to run. But if we stick with the friction, there can be a polishing, as we love each other and smooth out each other's rough spots, until we are like some highly burnished glass that can mirror the love of Christ to others.

When the Bible describes heaven, eternal life, our ultimate future with God, light blazes, and there is no darkness at all. Now we "see through a glass darkly, but then we will see face to face" (1 Corinthians 13:12). We will be able to look into the shining face of Christ and not be blinded, but healed. For "God is light, and in him is no darkness at all." The Psalmist wrote that God covers himself "with light as with a garment," prompting Charles Haddon Spurgeon to say, "The conception is sublime: but it makes us feel how altogether inconceivable the personal glory of the Lord must be; if light itself is but his garment and veil, what must be the blazing splendour of his own essential being."

John's vision of heaven, which God gave him while he was imprisoned on the island of Patmos, proclaimed hope and comfort to Christians persecuted for their faith, and to us today as we face uncertainty. His kaleidoscopic portrayal of the wonder of our life with God is shot through with light, light, more light.

> *And the city has no need of sun or moon*
> *to shine upon it,*
> *for the glory of God is its light,*
> *and its lamp is the Lamb.*
> *By its light shall the nations walk;*
> *and there shall be no night there.*
> — Revelation 21:23-25

Then we will have played out the great drama of life, which Dante understood well. Like him we find ourselves "in a dark wood, for I had wandered off from the straight path." Groping tirelessly, trying to escape the sorrows of the world, a surprise is hidden:

> *We climbed... until,*
> *through a small round opening ahead of us*
> *I saw the lovely things the heavens hold,*
> *and we came out to see once more the stars.*

At long last the poet reaches his goal, gazing into God's light, at home where we belong.

> *My eyes were totally absorbed in It...*
> *Then a great flash of understanding struck*
> *my mind, and suddenly its wish was granted.*
> *I felt my will and my desire impelled*
> *by the Love that moves the sun and the other stars.*

John's Gospel declares this was God's plan from the dawn of time: "In him was life, and the life was the light of men. The light shines in the darkness, and the darkness has not overcome it" (John 1:4-5).

And the darkness has not overcome it.

How the Light Gets In

Leslie B. Rindoks

There is evidence that Egyptians, as early as three millennia before Christ, were tinting, polishing and pressing glass for use in decorative objects. Stained glass as we know it today, pigmented and blown, surely grew out of that ancient art form. One of the earliest written accounts of stained glass is recorded in the ninth-century *Life of Ludger* where the following miracle is related: Amazingly, after spending a night at a saint's tomb, a blind pilgrim awoke the next morning able to "distinguish the images painted on the windows."

Throughout the Medieval Ages artisans lifted the craft to incredible heights as they created astounding windows for such cathedrals as Germany's Ausberg Cathedral, Paris' Sainte Chapelle and of course, Notre Dame.

Centuries ago worshippers who congregated in those vast churches continued to look upon stained glass as a miracle. Physics, as understood in the Dark Ages, stated that although the light of God was immaterial, the light emanating from the sun, moon and stars was matter. To their minds then it was indeed miraculous that the physical matter of light could pass through the physical matter of glass without shattering it completely.

Today, those same windows are still regarded as miracles, albeit for different reasons. Despite all our advanced tools and technology, modern day artists have yet to duplicate some of the intensely rich hues found in medieval stained glass windows.

The windows that help define the physical boundaries of Davidson United Methodist Church's sanctuary literally and figuratively "let in the light" and perhaps help bring about their own small miracles in the doing. As sunlight streams through, bringing each pane to life, a passage way for the light of God's word is provided and it shines upon all who enter this space.

In 1994, as the sanctuary interiors committee began the process of overseeing and guiding the design of these windows, we were faced with a challenge: To use a centuries-old art form, portray historical events and infuse the whole with meaning that is relevant for today. Working with the expert staff of the Willet Stained Glass Studios, we strove to make a theological statement that would articulate the relationship between this congregation and the ongoing Christian tradition. The results of our planning, debate and deliberation are windows that, individually are works of art, and when viewed collectively have even deeper meaning and power.

In the creation window (upper left in the sanctuary) exquisite design aesthetics combine with superb glass selection such that you can hear the gurgling essence of life itself surging forth. You can feel the energy bounding outward, bouncing across the width of the worship space to the star window in the upper right.

Here we are led to realize that this brightly shining star has not only guided wise men and shepherds, but is there to guide us today. We can go safely and with purpose into the world – if we but pause to *look up*.

In our quest to capture meaning for today's world, the series of saint windows do not stop at the Reformation with Martin Luther, but include John Wesley's contributions and Francis Asbury's journey to America; they courageously continue into the 20th century by celebrating

Mother Teresa and Martin Luther King.

The crucifixion theme for the rose window was determined early on and the committee felt strongly that this main window should not be a static depiction of an historic event. Rather than stating, "It is finished," it should instead proclaim, "In Him is life!"

No one committee member knew exactly what the window should look like, only that we "would know it when we saw it." As illustrated by the accompanying conceptual sketches, we explored many possibilities and it took some time before we "saw it." Through many revisions and reiterations we arrived at a representation of the crucifixion that is not at all traditional. The final design succeeds in not only looking back, but forward as well.

Other key ingredients were integral to the success of the sanctuary's fenestration. One that cannot be overlooked is the architecture itself. Bonson Hobson, WKWW Architects, designed a wonderful building that integrates window openings set to natural light on four elevations, each one requiring its own solution. Willett Stained Glass Studios interpreted the interiors committee's themes and design directions. Their talented team: Jane Collins, designer; Mirjam Seeger, glass painter; and Michael Susko, studio foreman worked in concert to bring to life windows that are both original in content and artistically compatible with the structure.

Spend time getting to intimately know these glass canvasses: Enjoy the early morning sunlight as it dapples the ceiling with pastel softness; behold the mid-day myriad of color that rains down from the rose window; walk up into the chancel and experience the sacrament windows that nestle there; witness first-hand how the light gets in – into our church and into our hearts.

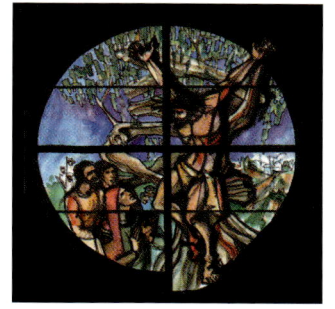

In one of Jane Collins' (of Willet Stained Glass Studios) earliest conceptual renderings the image of a gnarled and twisted olive tree played a prominent role. The design, while artistically successful, was too historic in its representation to accomplish our goal of looking to the future.

A later concept integrated free-form shapes around Christ. This idea began to approach what we were looking for, but we believed that more literal representations of people reacting and interacting would improve the design. This color palette and color sequence was used in the final design. At this stage the placement of the structural supports was finalized.

A subsequent design idea shows a major departure in style, demonstrating the broad scope of Jane's talent. While the rhythm of this design was appealing, we were looking for a more hopeful feeling and asked for an even more literal interpretation of the figures around the cross.

One of the last conceptual sketches shows nearly all the final elements in place. The overall color palette from the earlier submission sketch was revived and applied to this concept. The personality and the ethnicity of Christ was explored more deeply before the design process was completed.

Window Donors

The Creation Window was given by Frances L. Gwynn in honor of her daughters, Joanna C. Schachner and Ruth G. Shaw.

The Baptism Window was given by Mrs. Betty Billue Guignard in memory of her parents, J.V. and Tommy Bowers.

The Holy Communion Window was given by Debbie Ellis in honor of her parents, Lola and Bill Ellis.

The Rose Window was given by Ruth Hoyle Cathey in memory of her husband, William A. Cathey.

The Saint Windows

> Paul, Silas & Lydia was given by Alden Bryan in memory of his parents, Tom and Blanche Bryan.
>
> Francis & Clare of Assisi was given by Leah and Dale Ensor in honor of their parents, G. Howard Ensor and Ina J. Morton; their children Robert Steven Ensor, Jeffrey Scott Ensor, and Carol Ensor Jones; and in memory of their parents Gladys E. Ensor and Lester H. Morton.
>
> Martin Luther was given Anonymously in honor of the donors' Children and Grandchildren.
>
> John Wesley & Francis Asbury was given by Jean Fortner Ward, Ted Withers Fortner, and Martha Fortner McInnis in honor of their parents, Jim and Madge Fortner.
>
> Mother Teresa & Martin Luther King was given by Bob and Kathy Stark in honor of Dr. James C. Howell.

The Revelation Window was given by Jim and Bettie Smith in honor of her mother, Rosa Gant Torrence.